One hundred

LEGEND

BARRY MURPHY

WITH DOUG O'KANE

www.**HERO**BOOKS.digital

HEROBOOKS

PUBLISHED BY HERO BOOKS
1 WOODVILLE GREEN
LUCAN
CO. DUBLIN
IRELAND

Hero Books is an imprint of Umbrella Publishing
First Published 2020
Copyright © Barry Murphy and Doug O'Kane 2020
All rights reserved

ISBN 9781910827277

Cover design and formatting: jessica@viitaladesign.com
Ebook formatting: www.ebooklaunch.com
Photographs: The Murphy family collection

Dedication

For my wife Josy, my children Louise and Neil, and
Sally, Jack, Adam, Tom and David.

And the supporters of Barnsley Football Club.

Contents

Acknowledgements

IT HAS BEEN a pleasure ghostwriting Barry Murphy's book.

I knew Barry, of course, from interviewing him previously for the *Barnsley Chronicle*. Also, you can't spend any significant time around Oakwell, or the town's sporting scene, without knowing Barry Murphy.

But sitting down regularly with him during the last year and hearing his story in full has been a great experience.

I have paid many visits to his house near the town centre in Barnsley and interviewed him, with his wife Josy contributing valuable memories as well as teas, cakes and bacon sandwiches.

It has been a very fun process and I hope, that together, we have created a book that Barnsley fans and football supporters far and wide will enjoy.

This book is first and foremost the story of Barry's life but I also see it as a way of looking at the history of Barnsley Football Club through the 1960s, 70s and 80s and later, as well as an insight into the many ways football changed through his decades in the professional game.

To write this book, I have read the match reports from all 569 of Barry's Barnsley games, scoured the *Barnsley Chronicle* archives for any mention of his name, and interviewed a series of his former Oakwell teammates.

Barry has a good memory of his career and my role has been to explore that, while refreshing it with information from his many scrapbooks and also various archives.

When looking through the newspaper cuttings, most of the mentions seemed to be praising his defensive work, explaining how much he had improved since first arriving at the club and describing the countless goal-line clearances he made.

There are also many photographs of Barry as he became a well-known figure in the town.

Barry's name, often misspelt as Barrie, and once even as Larry, is so often printed alongside those of Eric Winstanley, Pat Howard and Eric Brookes – the famous back four from the 1967/68 promotion season which he looks back upon with great fondness.

I found out some fascinating things about the club such as the time Halifax Town manager, Alan Ball was threatened with 'a poisoned dart laced with cyanide' if he attended a match at Oakwell, and when Barnsley faced a Czechoslovakian side including Antonin Panenka, famous for chipping in a penalty in the 1976 European Championship final. A game against Crewe Alexandra in January, 1966 was delayed by 18 minutes due to a clash of kits, then for another 15 after one of the crossbars collapsed and had to be repaired.

THIS BOOK HAS been written during the 2019/20 season which the Reds spent battling against relegation from the Championship. It is clear to see how much each twist and turn in the fight against the drop has meant to Barry, who still attends every Barnsley home game in his role as a club ambassador and host of the Legends Suite.

When the Reds are playing away, he puts a radio on his shoulder and listens to BBC Radio Sheffield while sitting in his favourite armchair in front of Sky Sports News as the scores come in.

The first thing he always mentions when I see him – after his usual warm greeting – is the most recent match, the club's league position and their future prospects.

He is clearly still very much emotionally invested in the club he loves, like any other fan. He adores football and regularly mentions that, despite his happy memories of his playing days, 'the game is much, much better now'.

The writing process also took place at a time during which, unfortunately, several Barnsley legends and Barry's former teammates have died. They include the aforementioned Brookes as well as World Cup winner, Norman Hunter. It is clear to see how much those losses pained Barry while bringing back some cherished memories.

He speaks lovingly about Norman Rimmington, despite the stitches he received in his leg when one of the Oakwell stalwart's makeshift hurdles broke.

BARRY'S 16-YEAR PLAYING career with Barnsley began at Halifax Town in 1962 and ended at Torquay United in 1978, with some huge matches in-between including cup ties against famous top flight sides, as well as a promotion in 1967/68.

A lot of Barry's early adult life seemed to revolve around brown envelopes.

The kind that contained his weekly wages and would be left on his mother's table so she could pay the bills and, after Barry left home, the kind that contained a precious new contract offer every April or May.

There have been many setbacks too.

Barry's footballing career, or maybe even his life, could have ended when he was about five years-old and was thrown into a river by his two older brothers as a joke that went wrong.

Because of that, he never learned to swim and used to lock himself in his hotel room when the team travelled abroad for pre-season trips to avoid being thrown in to the swimming pool.

He might never have made it to Oakwell had his mother not nursed him through pneumonia following that incident, or had a scout for South Shields not spotted him when watching one of his teammates at his first club, Morrison Busty.

He was also devastated by the unexpected death of one of his close childhood friends.

Later, he was turned down by his hometown club, Consett following a trial, then missed a crucial penalty against them for South Shields in a title-deciding game, causing him plenty of ridicule. He still got the move to a professional club he had been seeking all of his life, however, when he was 22.

At Oakwell, he was helped by Barnsley stalwarts, Johnny Steele and Gordon Pallister having stern words with him during his tough first five years with the Reds.

His mid-twenties were a nerve-wracking period of being in and out of the first team and wondering if he would be released, a fear that intensified once he married his Josy and they had their children, Louise and Neil.

Eventually, after breaking into the first team regularly and surpassing the club's record for successive appearances, he was dropped when approaching 200 consecutive starts.

But he continued to be a regular, even playing 100 successive games again when he was 38 and the oldest player in the Football League.

He later moved to Leeds United with Allan Clarke, a decision that left him in tears and *left* his face on dartboards in local pubs while his children were heckled about it in school – but it is a choice he has never regretted as it allowed him to experience football at the highest level.

His time at Leeds was not as successful as he had hoped for.

One of his very few regrets is celebrating in the Oakwell dugout when visiting as a Leeds coach.

Although he saw the early careers of the likes of David Seaman, John Sheridan and Dennis Irwin, two of his lowest footballing moments came at Leeds.

They were relegated from the top flight in 1982 – just a few years after the glorious Don Revie era – and he was let go in '84.

The six months after his shock departure from Leeds were the hardest of his life, and that experience left him unwilling to go back into professional football except as Barnsley manager – a position he applied for but lost out to his old friend, Allan Clarke in 1985.

After some time on the dole, he was working in leisure centres less than a year after coaching Leeds United's first team.

However, that portion of his working life was one of the happiest.

AT PENISTONE LEISURE Centre he would fake awards for his staff to make sure the business appeared in the local press. His football coaching sessions were extremely popular, however, and attended by the likes of John Stones, who would become a £50million England star, and future Barnsley captains, Chris Morgan and Marc Roberts.

He also worked as a scout for Blackburn Rovers, York City and later

Nottingham Forest, where he had some amusing encounters with the legendary Brian Clough.

There was a harrowing incident when he was refused entry to the club where he is the record appearance-maker because he had 'watched them enough', then far worse when he witnessed the tragedy at Hillsborough in 1989.

There are some funny stories, like the time he celebrated the only promotion of his playing career on the balcony at Chester in 1968, amidst the directors and in front of thousands of travelling fans, in just his underpants as he had left his shorts in the dressing-room.

There is also the story of John Evans, one of the heroes of the 1967/68 promotion side, lying about his age to earn a move to Barnsley, as well as the tale of the Reds' squad getting caught taking a shortcut while on one of Jim Iley's brutal runs through the town.

Barry was an extremely superstitious man who would follow the same routine every matchday and during a game. He refused to tell reporters how old he was and none of them knew until the end of his playing career – something that is scarcely believable in the era of various online football databases.

He only played in a game shown on TV once, which is one more time than he claims he has taken a painkiller tablet as he prides himself on his physical fitness while admitting he has been lucky with his injury record.

Barry also describes the guidebooks the players used to receive before every season, telling them not to swim – no problem for the terrified Barry – and not to have sex after a Thursday evening. They had to ask the club's permission to do pretty much everything, including getting married or learning to drive.

He was sent off twice. Once for swearing at a referee in a friendly which ended his second long run of appearances and, the second time, for clattering Neil Warnock, who became Barry's Oakwell teammate and friend, before finding fame as a manager.

He has witnessed Britain during World War Two – playing in air raid shelters and collecting the family's rations. Incredibly, he can recall their ration book number off the top of his head, almost three-quarters of a century later.

He was also in Barnsley while it was the epicentre of the 1984-85 Miners' Strike, and his criticism of the club for not reducing miners' ticket prices is one of several forthright views in this book. Another is his annoyance, more than half a century after the event, at having to play a reserve game on the day that Denis Law, George Best and Bobby Charlton's Manchester United played at Oakwell.

Barry discusses some of the various scenes of his life at Oakwell, including being in a bath with *Kes* actor, Brian Glover, training with someone who put paperback books in his socks instead of shin pads and having a furious Trevor Aylott's shirt thrown in his face.

THIS IS ONLY the second book Barry has ever read, but I know he has enjoyed reminiscing about his life in Barnsley.

I would like to thank him for the opportunity to share his story.

I'd like to thank Barnsley FC historian, David Wood, and also Andy Goodwin, for checking various stats and putting me right on so many things, while also adding some interesting details.

Thank you again to Barry for picking me to write the book and to Hero Books for deciding that Barry Murphy's life and times as a professional footballer should be presented in this memoir.

I would also like to thank all those who added to the book, including Barry's family as well as Mick McCarthy, Neil Warnock, Eric Winstanley, Joe Joyce, Ian Banks, Allan Clarke, Eddie Gray, Alan Hill and Pat Howard. If that reads like a 'who's who?' of Barnsley and Leeds legends from the 1960s, 70s and 80s, it is because Barry's career was so long and illustrious.

It is testament to him that it has been extremely easy to speak to all of them and they have been more than happy to talk about Barry. He truly is one of the most popular men in football and I can understand why.

He remains an extremely popular figure in the town and, in 2019, won a 'Special Achievement' award at the Proud of Barnsley awards ceremony.

I hope you enjoy reading the book as much as Barry and I have enjoyed writing it.

Doug O'Kane
August, 2020

Introduction

Mick McCarthy's first professional season, as a teenager for his hometown club Barnsley, was the last in the playing career of Barry Murphy, who was 19 years his senior. McCarthy went on to play and manage at the World Cup with the Republic of Ireland as well as in the Premier League. He credits Barry's influence in his early years for helping him achieve such heights.

WHEN I GOT into the first team at Barnsley as an 18 year-old in 1977, Barry Murphy – who I always knew as Murph – was just starting his 16th and final season as a Reds player.

It's a name I always remember being associated with the club when I was growing up in the town, but then I got to know him when I became a youth team player.

I remember him passing 500 games, then 550, and thinking that I would love to beat his appearance record. I didn't even get halfway there. Eventually I got to 272 before I left for Manchester City in 1983.

I just about scraped a few more club games in my whole career than Murph played for Barnsley, but to have played 569 games for one club is amazing and that record will never be beaten.

I WATCHED HIM for a couple of years as an apprentice. We would play in the morning, then sit on the sidelines for the first team games. We used to clean the first team's boots and I am sure some of them went tramping through mud on purpose to make them even more dirty, but Murph wasn't like that.

He was the most senior player at the club, with the most appearances, so we automatically respected him.

He always had time for us as apprentices and would give us help and advice. Some older players would take the mickey out of apprentices all the time but Murph would always look after us.

Even then, in his late thirties, he was still by far the best trainer. He would always be one of the first out and last back, and he was constantly at the front when we went on runs. He was super fit and very enthusiastic. He was inspirational, especially to a young lad like me at that time.

When I got into the first team, I was playing next to him because I was at centre-back and he was the right-back. He still offered me a lot of help and advice

He was a very reliable and solid player and there were many times when I messed up and he pulled me out of a hole. I probably did it for him as well, now and then.

I can't remember all the exact things he said to me; I was 18 and I have headed a lot of balls and drunk a few pints since then. But I just remember him being hugely encouraging and never being critical or putting me down.

If I was doing something wrong, he might take me to one side and have a word in my earhole but, if I made a mistake in a game, he would be the first one to try to lift my spirits.

I used to room with Murph when we went to away games.

I think the manager, Jim Iley, or whoever decided things like that, probably put us together on purpose because they wanted me to spend time with a model professional like Murph and learn off him. There were a lot of players who would have a fag or pint the night before games but Murph would never do that.

I know his wife Josy. She became friends with my wife, Fiona.

He was just a really good bloke. And they are a great couple.

If you could follow his example of how he trained and how he looked after himself, you knew you would have a good career. Don't get me wrong, we all had a pint after games in those days – including Murph – but he was very professional.

As a young kid, just making my way in the game, he was the perfect person to grow up alongside. He set such a good example.

He loved a joke and he was great fun, but he was also a very reliable character and just a good human being. Everybody liked and respected him.

MURPHY RETIRED AFTER my first season in the first team. Then Allan Clarke became our manager, which was massive for the club and town.

I had followed Allan's career for years at Leeds United and with England.

He turned our club and team around. He brought some much-needed professionalism and discipline to Oakwell. He stopped us washing our own kits at home; we all got club suits and started meeting up for pre-match meals.

Clarkey must have seen something in Murph to make him one of his coaches, and he was so well-liked at the club and had so much knowledge that he moved into that role very easily.

He would always be having a joke with us which was a good foil for Allan who was quite strict.

They used to say that Allan had his Brian Clough days, when he would shout at players for having their hands in their pockets or other little things.

Murph was the antithesis of that and they worked very well as a partnership.

Allan was quite distant from the players whereas Murph was the one around us all the time on the pitch and in the dressing-room.

It just worked, as you can see by the results we got.

I have great memories of the 1978/79 promotion season.

When I was an apprentice, Barnsley never ever looked like getting a promotion. It was a troubled time for the club. I know that they had some success in the 1960s but, when I was growing up in the 70s, it wasn't a good era at Oakwell and I had never really seen them have success.

Under Jim Iley they were often a bang-ordinary team who were usually in mid-table or below that, and there were maybe three or four thousand fans in the ground most weeks. It was so quiet in the ground that you could clearly hear the shouts of 'ILEY OUT' and 'DENNIS OUT' and… 'LET'S HAVE A CLEAR-OUT' about the manager and the chairman, Ernest Dennis.

I remember, as apprentices, we used to laugh in the laundry room with Nelly and Nancy, who used to clean the kits.

We used to mimic the fans… but we'd shout 'NELLY OUT!' and 'NANCY OUT!'

Within a couple of years we suddenly went from that to having Allan Clarke as manager and getting promotion in front of crowds of about 15,000. It was lovely because it was the first time in my life that I had seen anything like that at Oakwell.

Barry and Clarkey left the next year for Leeds.

I still see Murph sometimes when I come back to Barnsley, and we have a catch up at Silkstone Golf Club.

There is no doubt that Barry had a great influence on my career and helped me get to where I eventually got in the game. To watch, play with, and then play under someone as reliable, responsible and passionate as him was a really good learning base for me.

You can see how much he is respected by all the fans and the club. He deserves to be the ambassador because he is a real, proper stand-up guy.

Mick McCarthy
August 2020

Prologue

IN THE MORE than one thousand football games I played in my life, from junior and non-league level in the North East, reserve football for Barnsley and 569 first team appearances, I gave one hundred percent – or one hundred and ten percent as I often say – in every single match. Apart from one.

It was a Barnsley reserves match at Bolton Wanderers in 1966.

Although I am known as the Reds' record appearance-maker, the first five years after I came down from County Durham to Barnsley were very challenging as I was never a first team regular.

Every year, from 1963 to '66, I had big doubts about whether I would be retained towards the end of the season. I faced an agonising wait to see that contract offer drop through the letterbox.

I got to 27 and was still mainly a reserve, so I thought that my dream of being a professional footballer was never going to be truly fulfilled.

I would get into the first team, then get dropped.

And that just kept happening, over and over again for several seasons.

MY TEAMMATES AND coaches would tell me I would get my chance and reassure me that I was doing a great job developing the younger players in the reserves, but that wasn't what I had got into football for.

I was questioning how long this could go on for.

The threat of being released became more worrying when I had a family to provide for.

On this particular occasion in 1966, I had broken into the first team and I thought I did quite well. But I got dropped and put back in the reserves, which was a real sickener.

I thought I deserved to stay in the side and I felt very down about my chances of ever being first choice.

Then I had to travel with the reserves to Bolton Wanderers.

My heart wasn't in it.

It's the first and only time in my life I didn't try my hardest at football.

Or, at anything.

We lost 6-2.

I was walking off the pitch when Gordon Pallister caught up with me. He was one of the club directors. He walked next to me.

Gordon was a North East man, like me. And he had played for Barnsley.

"You didn't enjoy that... did you?' he stated.

That's all he said but it made a big impact.

It must have been that obvious.

On the way back, I thought about it and decided that I was never going to play like that again and that, if I was going to fail at Barnsley, it wasn't going to be through me not giving absolutely everything I had to be in that first team.

I knew that the next time I got in the side, there was no way anyone was taking me out of it.

Luckily for me, there was a 'next time'.

And that 'next time' led to me breaking a series of records at the club, having a 16-year playing career in the Football League, then coaching in the top division in the country and, most importantly, making this town a home for me and my family.

WHEN I look back at the 278 games between March of 1967 and October of 1972, and think that I only missed one of them, I can't really believe it. I just loved playing football, the rhythm of being in the team every Saturday for years and years and the thrill of seeing my name on that team-sheet every matchday; then playing in front of the fans.

It was fantastic.

It just felt like I was living the life I had dreamed of when I was a football-mad little boy in my tiny home village.

At the time, I barely noticed as I passed 400… 450… 500…then 550 games. Neither did I fully understand what was happening when I broke the appearance records set by other club heroes, such as Harry Hough and my great friend, Eric Winstanley.

The local reporters used to remind me how many games I was on, but I didn't pay that much attention. I was just focused on playing football.

The records didn't mean that much at the time, but they mean a lot more now.

It didn't really sink in until after I retired.

Now, I think of it as a great honour.

I think of all the players who have graced the turf at Oakwell, many of whom have been a lot better than me, but I played more games than any of them.

I know I could play a bit, and I could defend well, and I suited all the managers I played under.

I get teased a bit sometimes that I only scored three goals in nearly 600 games, but that wasn't my job. I've been told that I had more goal-line clearances for the club than any player.

While my appearance record is there to be broken, I will always be the club's first substitute which is a quirky little statistic that I quite like. I came off the bench against Luton Town in October, 1965.

Having said it is there to be broken, I am very proud of my appearance record and I don't think it will ever be beaten, or the record of consecutive games.

That's because it is a different game now. A better game. When you see the facilities and the conditions today compared to when we played, it's totally different. There was no such thing as 'health and safety' when I played.

But there are other changes which mean that players don't stick around for long spells, like I did at Barnsley.

Agents are always talking to other clubs and trying to get their players more money, and move them away. We didn't have any of that when I was playing, so a lot of players just stayed at the same club.

The other reason is that managers change so often. I only played under three managers in 16 years at Barnsley and luckily all of them liked me. But these days, the managers change every other year, or sometimes more often, and they usually change the whole squad.

Another factor was my versatility.

Once I was established, managers always found me a place in the team, at right-back, left-back, centre-back or midfield, and I even played up front once or twice.

I was lucky not to get any bad injuries and I played in an era when, if you had an injury, you would try your best to get patched up and play. I was always a fitness fanatic.

I ran, I never smoked, I only drank a little bit, and ate as well as I could.

I have always taken two cod liver oil tablets every day, and that's it. I don't think I have ever even had a painkiller tablet. When I look back now and think that I did 15 or 16 pre-seasons, with the running they used to make us do, especially under Jim Iley, it was a very long time in football. But I loved every second of it.

'GRANDDAD… WE WANT 10 pence for everyone who stops you to talk about football when we go around Barnsley'.

When they were little, that's what my grandkids used to say to me.

Because I have been around the town so long, I've become quite a well-known face and I always love talking to fans.

I like to think the fans warmed to me because I have always been a battler who gives everything that he has to give.

I am still the same Barry Murphy as the one who came down from the North East nearly 60 years ago, but I have learned an awful lot from my time in my adopted home.

What I hope people get out of this book is to realise where I came from in the North East and that I always wanted to be a footballer. And that I managed to do that in Barnsley, which is my home now.

Signing for this club was the best thing I ever did.

I met my wife here, I have a lovely family, and I had a fantastic career with Barnsley Football Club.

PART ONE

Awakenings

PREVIOUS PAGE: My last day as a roof tiler (right); with my brothers, Brian and Thomas in the early days of my life as a professional footballer; and the happiest day of my life as I marry Josy in 1964.

« CHAPTER 1 »

I WAS BORN on February 10, 1940 in the village of Crookhall in County Durham and I lived there for the first 22 years of my life.

Crookhall is near the town of Consett in North West Durham and, in that era, there were two jobs a man from there could realistically do.

You could go down the mines, like my father did for 50 years, or you could work at Consett Iron Company.

They were your only real options.

There were no universities or colleges when I finished school. It was the mine or the steelworks.

But I saw a third option.

I ALWAYS WANTED to be a professional footballer.

I used to watch my father and brother go off to work and come back exhausted, and I desperately didn't want to do that.

When my father came back from work, he was usually totally covered in soot, black from head to toe. We had a big tin, free-standing bath and he'd go straight in there to get clean.

I'll never forget the time he came home and told me that he'd been working all day in a coal seam that was just a yard wide. I imagined what it would be like to spend a whole day down there in such a small space, working so hard, then doing it again the next day and the next for the rest of your working life.

I respect everyone who did that kind of work, but I knew it wasn't for me and it did give me extra motivation to make it as a footballer.

Everybody thought I would end up down those mines as well, or at the steelworks. A lot of people accepted it and followed their father, but not me. Of course, I was lucky that I was born with a talent for playing football.

I tell my grandsons now, as they go off to university, that my qualifications were in my feet.

AS SOON as I could walk, I played football.

My brothers were never that interested in it but my dad was and he had played a bit too. That's probably where my love of the game came from.

There was a field at the bottom of our street. It was a big open space four doors down from us with a full football pitch on it. I was there every day, whether I had people to play with or not. If there were 10 spare minutes in the day, between school and helping my mother out, I would go down there and kick a ball about.

I was a football fanatic and worshipped the sport.

My friends and I couldn't afford footballs, unless someone had given us one for Christmas, so we would play with tennis balls or whatever we could find.

On a Sunday afternoon, all the husbands in the village used to come home from the pub to eat their dinner; then meet at that pitch for a game of football.

I started to play with them as I got a bit older, and I'd hold my own, even at the age of 12 or 13. At first they put me in goal and gave me the nickname 'Sam Bartram' – he was the Charlton Athletic 'keeper and a very famous footballer at that time.

I once went down there on Christmas Day, after getting a football as a present, and tried to kick it around in two foot of snow. That's how obsessed I was. I learned the game on that pitch.

IT WAS EITHER Sunderland.

Or Newcastle.

In the area I grew up in, that was the choice. You did not support any other team. There were busloads going to both grounds from all the villages every weekend.

My father was a big Newcastle United fan and he used to take me to games at St James' Park. If we came in late, other fans would put the children on their shoulders and pass us down to the front.

I once went to see a game there against Manchester United.

They put us up on the top of the old scoreboard. It was tens of metres up in the air. There were about a dozen kids on the top of this scoreboard, half terrified and half excited, looking over this top flight football game and a crowd of 70,000 people. The only other people up there were the men who used to change the cards with numbers on as the goals went in. It was hellish if you looked down beneath your feet. It was better to just focus on the game.

It was the era of Jackie Milburn – 'Wor Jackie', who was my hero – and Bobby Mitchell, Frank Brennan, Jimmy Scoular, Joe Harvey and the Robledo brothers, who had come from Barnsley, which I didn't realise until later. Newcastle had a very good team in those days and won the FA Cup in 1951, '52 and '55.

The main games I remember were the FA Cup finals.

We didn't go to them; the idea of travelling down to Wembley was unthinkable for a family like ours at that time.

We didn't have a television either, so we had to go to the house of a family at the bottom of our street, who were more posh than us. We all used to cram into their front room and watch the Toon. Seeing those games at Wembley just made me more determined to be a footballer when I grew up.

I was always thinking about Newcastle and all my birthday and Christmas presents were books about the club, or socks or scarves in black and white colours.

My ambition was always to play for Newcastle.

The closest I got was when I got injured when I played for South Shields. They didn't have a physio so they used to send their injured players to St James' Park. I loved going there, even if it was just for a few hours as an injured non-league player.

THE HOUSE I grew up in was 21 Fourth Street. It sounds like an address from an American city but it couldn't have been in a more English, working class village.

Crookhall was a fantastic place, a very close community.

There were six streets of 24 terraced bungalows on my estate and I lived in one with my parents and two older brothers, Brian, who is six years older than me, and Thomas, who was five years older. My dad was Thomas as well and my mum was Elizabeth, but most people called them Tom and Lilly.

It was a massive house with a big backyard. Brian still lives in that house.

I was born at home. All the neighbours were there, which they were for every birth in the village in those days. It was a very tight-knit community and everyone looked after each other. Several of my mother's friends always used to tell me, 'I was the first to hold you'.

In the village there was a Co-op and a Post Office at the top of the street, and the football pitch at the bottom.

It wasn't easy at times but we were a very close family and, in truth, I had a lovely childhood.

We didn't have much money but we didn't feel deprived because no one else had anything more than us – only the man at the bottom of the street, who had a television. But he'd invite us in and let us watch the cup final, so that was fine.

I have some fond memories of those times. My father used to go running a lot and, as I got older, I went with him when I could to build up my fitness.

We used to have terrible weather up there. One night, when it was snowing really hard, my father fell over on his way home. He tripped over the top of a six-foot high bus stop sign which was almost totally buried in the whiteness.

I was the youngest of the three brothers so I used to get all the worst jobs to do. I was always the one who had to collect the coal when it got delivered and put it away. I was the one who did all the washing with my mother, and all the shopping and running about. That was a lot of my early life.

My brothers used to pick on me a bit. I was always the one who had to get the cigarettes from the shop, even though I was the only one who didn't smoke.

We were brought up disciplined. It didn't do us any harm and it made sure I was a hard worker, which stood me in good stead for the rest of my life.

I WAS BORN a few months after the start of World War Two. There were air raid shelters in the back gardens of all of the houses in Crookhall.

The German planes used to target the Consett Iron Works because they were creating a lot of valuable materials for the war effort. I can remember planes flying very, very low over Crookhall. Looking back now, they were very scary times but, at that age, you didn't realise the consequences.

Mineworkers were a protected profession so my father didn't have to go to war, but he was in the Home Guard. He had all the equipment… the uniform, the helmet.

He was always on standby for if the worst happened and we were invaded. When we heard the sirens, we all had to dash into the shelters. I was only little but I can remember getting carried in, and seeing everyone rushing about and looking worried.

Everyone sat on two benches in the shelter, and faced each other.

I don't really remember being scared because I didn't fully understand what was going on.

We would also play in the air raid shelters when they weren't in use and, for the first few years of my life, they were just part of our little world.

There was rationing during the war and for years afterwards.

We had ration books with coupons for milk, butter, meat and everything else.

A man from the Co-op would come around on Monday and take our order; then we would collect it on a Thursday morning. After the war, when I was a little bit older, it would be my job to collect the rations before school. I was sitting on the step every Thursday morning at 8am.

Every home had a number for their account. I remember ours off the top of my head even now, 70 years later… 2242.

There wasn't much to go around in those days. Luckily my mum was a very good cook and she used to make sure we always had enough.

She would bake bread every Tuesday. We could smell it on the windowsill when we were coming home from school. Those were good days.

I have a lot of happy memories from that part of my life because we had such a good family and the village of Crookhall was full of wonderful people.

NOT EVERYONE IN my childhood was so wonderful, however.

The school I went to, St Patrick's Catholic School in Consett, was run by nuns. And they were really strict.

My oldest brother, Brian was working at the steelworks and my mother used to make his sandwiches. Sometimes, if we had run out of bread, I had to go to the shop to get it first thing in the morning, then take his sandwiches to where he worked, then peg it to school.

Brian had to come first because he was putting that brown envelope on the table on a Friday night to help feed the family and I wasn't because I was just a schoolkid. That was the order of things and the way it had to be, to keep a roof over our heads and food on the table.

When I got to the steelworks with Brian's sandwiches, I used to stand on top of one of the furnaces and shout his name until he came to get his lunch.

It was a five-mile walk.

One day, I didn't get into school until after 10am.

The nun who ran the school knew I was late and took me up to her office. She hit me five times with the cane on each hand. She brought the cane back over her head and swung very hard. There were big red marks on my hands for days. I was about 10 or 11 years-old. I was never late again.

Brian could forget about his sandwiches.

That was the only time I really got into trouble. But I wasn't a good student at school. I can remember being in classrooms and just thinking about football, desperate to be outside.

MY FOOTBALL WAS always more important to me and it obviously worked out for me in the end.

On a Friday afternoon, the headteacher would always put the school team up on the wall. I didn't turn up for my lessons every day, but I would make sure I turned up that day because I always wanted to play in the games.

I was a good player at school.

There was another lad, Glyn Williamson, who thought he was better.

We decided to play a one-on-one game to decide who was the best. We were about nine years-old. All the pupils surrounded us and were shouting us on.

Someone threw the ball up in the air.

We started.

If you beat the other one, you would score.

Anyway, I won quite comfortably and I was the undisputed best player in the school at St Patrick's after that.

« CHAPTER 2 »

NOT LONG AFTER I kicked a ball for the first time, my football career was nearly over.

I was only about four or five years-old and it was during the six-weeks summer school holidays. Our mother used to give us some sandwiches and water, then myself and my two brothers would go out for the day.

This particular day, we went down to the River Derwent, where my brothers threw me in. They thought it was funny but it nearly went badly wrong. I had no idea how to swim.

I was in there for a good few seconds and swallowed a lot of water. It was extremely frightening. I was just waving my arms and kicking my legs and choking on the water, which was very cold even though it was summer.

I got out but I was in a real state when I got home, shivering and soaking. I was really unwell afterwards for weeks. My mother nursed me through it.

After a few days, a doctor came to our house and told us it was pneumonia. A fire was put on around the clock.

I had to sweat it out.

I HAVE OFTEN had a slight chesty cough ever since the river incident but it never affected my football. I know that if my mother hadn't looked after me as well as she did, I might not have been healthy enough to become a footballer.

She was a miner's wife and she was good at taking care of people. I owe her a lot.

But my fear of water was never cured and, to this day, I can't swim.

I kept that a secret but, about 30 years later, it nearly caught up with me when I was a player and first team coach of Barnsley. I took Jim Iley's team on a pre-season trip to Benidorm in Spain.

Jim didn't like flying so myself and the coach, Mick Buxton were in charge of the team.

We were staying in a big hotel with a large swimming pool. After training, I just locked myself in my room on the third floor and didn't tell anyone I couldn't swim. I knew that if they knew, they would throw me in because that was the kind of thing we used to do to each other. Kenny Brown, one of the other players, couldn't swim either so they threw him in.

He went down, came back up, went down again and they had to pull him out. I was watching through the curtains in my sanctuary three floors up, thinking about my brothers throwing me into the Derwent.

I was genuinely worried about drowning if I told anyone I couldn't swim.

I was thinking about the headline:

"PROFESSIONAL FOOTBALLER DROWNED BY TEAM-MATES ON HOLIDAY".

I laugh about it a lot when I look back on that now but it felt serious at the time.

I had tried to learn to swim. Me and another player, George Boardman used to go to swimming lessons at Royston Baths.

We had 12 sessions and I probably wouldn't drown if I went into some water now.

But I still can't swim.

THE ONLY OTHER thing I was interested in as a boy, as well as football, was training homing pigeons.

The lad I shared the loft with was called Alan Lumley, who lived near me on Fifth Street.

He was a big kid and a weight-lifter.

We once had some young pigeons and gave them to some lads we were working with, to let them out. We thought they would find their way back. It was a training exercise for them. But these lads let them off when it was pouring down with rain; you couldn't see a hand in front of your face.

We never got a single one of those pigeons back. I was furious with the lads who had let them off, because Alan and I had dedicated a lot of time to them.

We got some more and kept it up for a few years.

One day, Alan was going into hospital to have his appendix out and he told me to feed the pigeons while he was out of action. Later in the week, I was walking down the road with some bird food when I met a man we knew.

'Sad about your mate, isn't it?' he said.

I had no idea what he was talking about but he told me that Alan had never woken up from his operation. He was only 21. I was devastated.

I threw the food into the street and went home.

It killed me inside and broke my heart. He was a really close friend of mine and we went everywhere together. I'll never forget him.

We had a brand-new loft for the pigeons, but my heart just wasn't in it after that. I found them new homes and never kept any again.

I PLAYED FOR Crookhall Juniors. But in my teens, I moved on to High Gate Juniors in a nearby village.

I was only about 14 or 15 but I played centre-back against strikers who were 18 or 19. I was a thin lad but I knew I was faster than them, and I always held my own. I could look after myself.

When you play against older people, you develop physically and that was a time when I shot up in height as well.

The coaches wouldn't have played me at that level at centre-half if I wasn't physically strong.

I got poached by another local club called Morrison Busty, an unusual name that always makes me laugh. It was there that I started playing for the men's team, and that's when I got my big break in 1959 when I was 19 years-old.

I had already had a trial at Consett but they turned me down. It was really disappointing because they were my home town and they played in the Northern Counties League, which would have been a great opportunity for me. That just made me want to work harder and I tried not to doubt myself, even though it was a knock back.

Eventually I got another chance.

The manager of South Shields, Charlie Thomas was watching a lad called Joe McCabe, a centre-forward who was scoring goals for fun for Morrison Busty. But Joe had a bad game and I had a good one at centre-back. I caught Charlie's eye. He wanted to see me afterwards and I signed for South Shields.

That was the turning point in my career, and my life.

If Charlie had gone to another game that day or if I'd had a bad match or Joe had had a good one, I might never have been spotted and might have ended up down the mines. But I was in the right place at the right time.

SOUTH SHIELDS WAS 30 miles away but my older brother, Brian took me to training on Tuesday and Thursday evenings, and to games on a Saturday. My parents couldn't drive but Brian had a car.

It was a great standard. It was the best semi-professional league in the area and probably the best in the country, with a lot of players going on to play professionally. A lot of the lads had already played for Football League clubs. The North East was a real hotbed of football talent.

Lawrie McMenemy, who went on to manage Southampton and win the FA Cup, was manager of Gateshead, who were in the league below us at the time, then later Bishop Auckland.

I have read his autobiography. It's the only book I've ever read, and he mentions a lot of the teams that I played for and against during that time.

South Shields was a big club with decent facilities. They wanted to get into the Football League and applied but never managed it. We got to the first round of the FA Cup in 1961.

At that stage I used to get expenses, but no wages.

Our ground was called Simonside Hall and we used to get good crowds of 3,500 to 4,000.

That was, in some ways, the biggest step up of my career in terms of facilities and atmosphere because, at Morrison Busty, we were just playing in front of a few people and we didn't even have any linesmen.

After being in and out of the side in my first season, I broke into the team in the 1960/61 campaign due to an injury and stayed there for the next two years.

I began to develop quickly and made a decent reputation for myself.

One of the articles in the local press said, *"If you want a centre-back in the North East, you go to South Shields and get Barry Murphy"*.

It was fantastic because I had worked all my life for this.

But it wasn't all plain sailing.

South Shields were in the Northern Counties League, as were my home town club Consett.

There wasn't too much aggro towards me when I went out in Consett on the weekends, mainly just banter.

Us and Consett were competing at the top of the league one season and we played each other in a crucial match. We got a penalty and I was the taker even though we had some semi-pro lads and I was only a teenager.

I had taken all the penalties all season and done well. But I missed that one.

The headline in the local *Consett Chronicle* the next week was, *"Murphy gives Consett the chance of winning the league"*. They did win the league by a couple of points and I got a bit of stick from the South Shields fans for costing them the title, and from the people in Consett as well.

It was frustrating at the time but I was never someone who let things like that get to me. I was so focused on making it as a professional that I knew I just had to move on to the next game.

I HAD OPTIONS to play for other clubs. You could sign for as many teams as you wanted, as long as they weren't in the same league.

West Auckland were going to Wembley for a cup final and they wanted me to play for them there as a one-off, which I could have done as they were in a different league. I turned them down. It was my only chance to play in the national stadium but I don't regret it, because I wanted to stay loyal to South Shields.

The only other senior team I played for at that time was Durham County FA at Lincoln City's Sincil Bank. I have still got the badge at home. I played for South Shields and then, the next day, I travelled down to Lincoln to play for the county. Durham would go on to win the Northern Counties Amateur Championship.

AS WELL AS my football, I worked Monday to Friday when I was up in the North East.

You had to have a brown envelope to put on the kitchen table on a Friday night. That was the mantra in our house.

My mother would collect the envelopes from my father, my brothers and me and use that money to pay for rent, food and everything else. We would get £1.50 pocket money; my father got £2.50.

We went to the working men's club for a few pints and cigarettes until our money was gone.

I got my first job when I was 15 years-old, which is when I left school. I was delivering coal from coal merchants to people's homes. I used to carry a 100-weight bag of coal. I was only a skinny lad.

My boss, Johnny Walker would carry two of them at a time, and I'd carry one. But I got paid for it and I had a brown envelope to take home at the end of the day. It stood me in good stead and toughened me up a bit. I definitely became stronger doing that job, which helped me in my football, but it's a bit different to the weight training players do now.

Then I had four years as a tiler. We would put roofs on houses, churches, cinemas, any type of building.

I was once on the top of the Empire Cinema in Consett and it looked over the whole village. My mother walked across the market down below. There were no shops in Crookhall, so she had to go into Consett to buy what we needed.

'MOTHER... MOTHER,' I shouted down at her.

She had the fright of her life. Then she noticed I was standing right on the edge of this building about 40 or 50 feet in the air.

'GET DOWN...

'GET DOWN... NOW!' she shouted back up at me.

She wasn't happy with me when I got home.

My first boss as a tiler used to have a truck with a canopy on the back.

One day, they didn't have the canopy and I refused to get on. It was the middle of winter and it was very cold.

I could be quite stubborn. We had a row and I quit.

I was too scared to go home and tell my mother I had lost my job so I got on my bike and cycled about six miles to another business, and they took me on. If they hadn't had a job for me, I would have just kept looking until I could go home without being in trouble.

When I got my contract with Barnsley, my tiling boss was called Pat Hughes and he offered me half the business to stay and work with him. I was never going to do that.

No one would have changed my mind.

The *Consett Chronicle* got a picture of my last day working on the roofs before becoming a full-time footballer.

SCOUTS FROM PROFESSIONAL clubs had started to watch me.

West Bromwich Albion, Wolverhampton Wanderers, Darlington, Hartlepool and some others.

I had a reputation as the best up-and-coming player in the North East, or that is what the papers called me anyway.

It made me a bit nervous to know the scouts were in the crowd but, when it's what you want to do, you try a bit harder.

Next thing, the scouts started to knock on the door of the house.

My mum made sure that all the best cups and saucers came out of the cupboards for their visits. Wolves offered me a deal and so did Barnsley, who had identified me through their North East scout, Harry Nattrass.

Johnny Steele and Norman Rimmington, the Barnsley coaches, came to visit me. They would become two very important figures in my career and my life. Johnny had been up in Scotland on holiday and called at Newcastle on his way back to sign me.

We met at the Station Hotel in Newcastle.

They sold the club to me with their passion and the way they spoke about the game.

One of the reasons I picked Barnsley was because it was very similar to home. It was the same sort of community, all based around mining. Consett Colliery Band was famous around the country, just like Grimethorpe Colliery Band from Barnsley.

Also, a lot of people from Consett came down to work in Barnsley when they shut the mines up there.

It just seemed like the right club to join, and I certainly picked a winner.

My mother worked behind a bar in Consett and, after I signed for Barnsley, I went straight to see her. She was glad for me because she knew it was all I ever wanted, but she was sad that I would be leaving home. Not long after, Brian dropped me off.

And that was it.

I was a Barnsley player.

« CHAPTER 3 »

MY BROTHER LEFT me with my suitcase and went back up to the North East. I had never been away from home before.

I didn't really know what I was doing.

The club had put me in digs with four other players, not far from the town centre. I introduced myself to my new flatmates, then went down to the ground to have a look. It was a proper Third or Fourth Division ground at that time. But the facilities were more than adequate for what we needed.

I remember seeing two players called Bobby Wood and Frank Bartlett, who had just finished running and were comparing how many laps they had done of the training pitch.

'I've done 23,' said one.

'Well... I've done 25,' came the reply.

I was introduced to them and I knew I was in for some hard work.

They were two lovely lads and stalwarts of Barnsley Football Club at that time. They always had time for me even though I was a young lad in the reserves.

Bartlett was from Chester-le-Street in the North East. He was the club's top-scorer at the time but he was always good to me.

On my first day of training I met all the players, then I got my place in the dressing-room. All the senior lads used to use the home dressing-room and the apprentices were in the away dressing-room.

We trained from 10am to 12 noon every weekday, except Wednesdays; unless we had a bad result, then we were in every day including Sundays.

We used to get our kit out of the drying room and, if you were lucky, you got the same one as the day before.

Training was nothing like it is now. It was a lot of running and none of the technical work that modern footballers do. We trained in all weathers.

When the snow was on the ground and we couldn't train outside, we used to do shuttle runs up and down the steps of the stands inside the stadium. It was a fantastic education and lads don't have that now.

I was a trainer's dream.

They used to put me at the front of the run and say, 'Keep up with Murph'. All the older, married lads would be lagging behind and shouting at me, 'For God's sake Barry... SLOW DOWN LAD!'

But that's who I was.

I always had the same thought in the back of my mind. It's either this... or the mines or the steelworks. Whenever I felt my legs hurting, I would think about that and I'd keep going.

It was a dream come true to be a footballer and to be paid to train and kick a ball about.

I WAS ON £20 per week at first, which was decent money in those days and much, much more than what I had been on as a tiler.

We also got £4 for a win, and £2 for a draw.

If we got a crowd of 10,000, we got an extra £1. And if it was 14,000, we got £2. But that didn't happen very much at that time.

In the reserves, it was £2 a win and £1 after a draw.

The first team got bonuses for league position as well; a little bit extra if we were in the top four. When we were high up in the table, we were excited because we might be getting promoted, but we would also get a little bit more money.

I would send £3 or £4 up to my mother every week, which went a long way. Even though I was away from home, I still wanted to make sure I put that brown envelope on her table every week. What I had left lasted me easily.

All of the players paid 50 pence a week into an account at Jackson's the Tailor, where Yorkshire Building Society is now in Barnsley, until we wanted something like a suit and it was paid for.

All the players lived in the town.

We used to play snooker quite a lot at a club in the town centre after training.

The older players like Frank Bartlett and Bobby Wood used to hang around near the bus station, then go down to a betting shop on Eldon Street in the town centre.

Sometimes we would go down with them; not to have a bet, because we couldn't afford it.

At weekends, we went out on the town together too. We saved our money for that.

If we had a good result, it was… 'Look out Barnsley… HERE WE COME!'

WHEN I FIRST moved to Barnsley, I lived in digs with my teammates, George Kerr, Alan Hopper, Hughie Cochrane and Walter Gerrard.

The house was owned by a woman called Mrs Spensley, who lived there as well. In the digs you would get breakfast and an evening meal provided by the landlady.

We all got on well and I enjoyed living there.

The only problem was that there were half a dozen cats in the house and I am not really a cat person.

Myself and George Kerr tried to avoid all these cats the best we could. But, apart from that, it was a good place to live. Hughie didn't make it at Barnsley in the end but he was a big friend of mine at that time.

He and I later moved to a different house in Beech Street in Worsbrough with a landlady called Mrs Williams. She was fantastic. She was a professional chef so she used to cook us some very nice meals.

The only problem was that she fed us too well so we had to watch what we ate. I always tried to make sure that I ate healthily as a footballer but I didn't want to upset Mrs Williams by turning her food down. I have good memories of that first experience of being away from home and starting to make my way in the game and in Barnsley.

BARNSLEY, AS A town, was more or less like the town of Consett, and the people were very similar as well.

I did struggle with the accent and the way of speaking. I walked into a fish and chip shop, for instance, a few weeks after I moved.

There was a big queue.

'Fish and a bag,' I asked when it was my turn.

They just looked at me.

They had no idea what I wanted.

I had to learn to say, 'Fish and chips once'.

There must have been five or six of us from the North East at Oakwell in those days. It was good to have other people at the club who were from the same part of the country as me.

There were semi-professionals in the squad like Bob Earnshaw, who was a schoolteacher but used to train in the evenings. There was always a lovely family atmosphere at the club.

WE GOT GIVEN little books every year telling us the rules of the club.

We weren't allowed to buy a car without the club's permission.

We also had to get permission to learn to drive.

We had to get permission to get married.

We weren't allowed to swim because we would be using different muscles to playing football. I couldn't swim anyway, so that wasn't a problem.

No sex was allowed after Thursday night.

They were very different times.

WHEN I FIRST came down from the North East, I used to go home every weekend to see family and friends. But one weekend when I came back to Barnsley there was a knock on my door.

I was told the manager, Johnny Steele wanted to see me.

'Your living is here now... not the North East,' he told me.

'You need to settle here.'

They were wise words from a very, very wise man. It just clicked for me straight away and I made a life in Barnsley after that. If I wanted to be a footballer for my whole career, I had to commit to this club and this town.

JOHNNY WAS MY first manager at Oakwell.

He was a football man and the club meant a lot to him.

He had started off as a part-time coach two nights a week and then got promoted to the first team coach.

He was a Scotsman, but he seemed to have a really strong connection to Barnsley. Johnny was also a smashing coach. If results weren't going for him, he would have words with us like any coach, but he was fair.

He was the one who moved me to right-back, having been a centre-back all my career. I am not exactly sure why he decided to move me. He obviously saw something I didn't. He tried me in a few different positions early on but eventually I broke into the team at right-back and made that position my own.

You had to be a better defender at right-back than centre-back, because you were always playing against very fast wingers. You had to have a lot of pace to keep up with them, but I was always capable of that.

I had to learn to look around all over the pitch at full-back whereas, at centre-back, I only really looked in front of me.

These days, full-backs get forward on the attack but, when I played, you weren't encouraged to do that as much and the only job of the back four was to defend.

BARNSLEY'S RESERVES IN the 1960s played in the Central League, and they weren't very good.

When I first came to the club, I was mainly a reserve player and we used to lose nearly every game. If we got a draw, we would go out and celebrate.

We would never get relegated or thrown out of the league because our chairman, Joe Richards was also the president of the Football League. He made sure we stayed in the Central League every season.

Chesterfield also had a chairman who was quite high up in the FA, so the same thing happened to them. It was always a battle between the two of us to avoid finishing last but, unfortunately, it was usually Barnsley who propped up the table at the end of the season.

I don't like losing so, at times, it was very difficult. But I learned a hell of a lot from those first years, which I put into practice when I eventually got into the first team.

It was a fantastic standard in the Central League. We came up against a lot of big clubs with big squads who fielded some better sides in the reserves league than some of Barnsley's first team opponents in the Third and Fourth Divisions.

Clubs used the reserves to get players back to fitness after injuries so sometimes I did come up against big names. I marked Everton's Johnny Morrissey, who played hundreds of games for them in the top flight and helped them win the title a couple of times. I pulled my hamstring chasing after him, one of the only times I ever got injured.

We also played against a Wolves team with nine internationals in it. And we went to Old Trafford to play Manchester United. Alex Stepney was in goal, and there were about 15,000 supporters in the stands.

We would get about 1,000 supporters for some of our home games.

I improved a lot in those first few seasons because the standard of training and the games, even in the reserves, was much higher than I was used to. I was training every day and coaches like Norman 'Rimmo' Rimmington helped me a lot.

◄ ◄ ◆ ▷ ►

Barry Murphy reflects on his friend, Norman Rimmington, who spent more than 70 years at Oakwell as player, coach, groundsman, physio and kitman. Norman passed away in 2016.

SOME PEOPLE CALL me 'Mr Barnsley' because of my appearance record but Norman Rimmington is the only person who deserves that nickname.

Norman worked at the club for 70 years, from the 1940s until just before his death in 2016. He really should have had a book written about him because he had so many wonderful stories. He is a total legend in the town.

Norman was born and bred in Barnsley and he always wanted to be a player, then a coach, at the club. He achieved that and more after a stint as a miner.

The first time I met Norman was when he had just been appointed as Johnny Steele's coach and they both came to meet me in Newcastle.

Norman was so enthusiastic about the club and the things they had planned, it convinced me to move to Barnsley.

He was the senior coach and it was his first coaching job. When I arrived at Oakwell, he was the one who did a lot of the training although, in those days, it was mainly running and fitness work.

A few weeks after I joined, we went to watch a match at Leeds United against Crystal Palace, who we were playing not long afterwards. I was sitting next to Rimmo. At the end he asked me if I enjoyed the game?

'Yes,' I told him. 'But I couldn't understand a word you said.'

He was broad, broad, broad Barnsley.

He said, 'inside forrud' instead of 'forward'… 'centre heerf' instead of 'half'… 'are tha oreyt?' to check if you were 'OK'… and 'si thi' instead of 'goodbye'. I couldn't understand a word of it, and he was probably the same with what I was saying.

But Norman looked after me when I first came down to Barnsley.

He was always supportive of me when my career wasn't going the way I wanted it to and I wasn't getting in the first team. He used to say I was a trainer's dream and he would always give me encouragement when I needed it.

One day, Norman decided he wanted to change our training regime instead of just doing lap after lap after lap of running. He made some hurdles out of cane and put them together with tape and a few nails.

He took us to a bit of wasteland where the car park is now at Oakwell. It used to belong to Barnsley Brewery but we could use it if we wanted.

It was very bumpy, uneven ground but he put these rickety hurdles out and got us to run along and jump over them. He would test our pulse after each run.

It all came to an end when I tried to jump over the second one but didn't clear it properly. I stood on the top of his hurdle and it gave way under my weight. I fell straight down on top of it and a splinter cut the inside of my leg.

There was blood all over the grass. I was taken to hospital and had to have stitches in the wound. Apparently, I fainted but I can't really remember.

That was the last time we used those hurdles, and we laughed about it afterwards.

Norman threw them in the bin. 'I thought it was a good idea but I was wrong,' he admitted. 'Forget about it.'

He always meant well for the club and his heart was in the right place.

Luckily it was pre-season so I didn't miss any games and, once the wound had healed up, I was back in action.

Later on, Norman became our groundsman – taking over from Albert Brookes the father of Eric Brookes – then, after Allan Clarke arrived in 1978, he was made physiotherapist, something he had done previously when he was our coach. He had qualifications and he learned a lot from other people.

It wasn't like physiotherapy is now, because it has become a real science. But Norman did know a lot and he was good at any job he did for the club.

If you had a minor injury, he would convince you that you were fully fit and you would be playing the next game.

All the players wanted to go into the physio room just to talk to him and get some advice. He was a very calming presence and you always left that room feeling better than when you went into it.

Rimmo was like a father figure to all the players.

You could have a joke with him, and he liked that.

Me and Big Eric used to torture him.

One game, we travelled up to Hartlepool and Norman had a bit of an injury which meant he couldn't walk very well at the time.

The team bus picked him up from his house in Darton.

We told him on the bus that no one would get injured and he wouldn't have to move from the bench all afternoon.

Then, during the game at different times, both myself and Eric pretended to be injured in the farthest corner of the pitch so he had to run across to the farthest part of the ground. We were secretly giggling about it.

It was a bit cruel. He gave us stick about that for the rest of his life but he did see the funny side.

If anyone had a bad game, got sent off or made a mistake, Norman would tell him what he thought about their performance in his usual forthright way but then somehow manage to cheer them up as well.

He told so many stories about his days down the mines and the players he played with, like George Robledo.

He spoke a heck of a lot of sense.

Even the directors would come and talk to Norman about what he would do. They often took his advice on hiring new managers.

All the managers I played for wanted to get Norman's advice. He was always going down to the national training centre in Lilleshall to get his latest qualifications. He was so enthusiastic for the game. All the ex-players who would come back would always make a bee-line to see Norman.

He had a very close relationship with Mick McCarthy for many years and Mick made an excellent speech at Norman's funeral.

His funeral had a massive turnout and rightly so. Everyone wanted to pay their respects to a wonderful man.

I always kept in touch with Norman and myself and Josy went to see him in a care home towards the end. It was so sad to see a man like Norman Rimmington finish in that way.

He was lovely man and his wife Jessie was a lovely woman. It had hurt him a lot when she had died a few years before.

Everybody in football liked Norman Rimmington, which you can't say about many people.

He was part of the fixtures and fittings of the stadium and the club.

He was a very proud Yorkshireman.

There aren't many people who have worked at one club for 70-odd years.

He is very, very well respected in the town and there is a bar named after him at Oakwell.

I can't speak too highly of him and I miss him a lot.

◂◃◆▹▸

BARNSLEY FANS MIGHT know me now as the club's all-time top appearance-maker, but some of them may not realise that, for the first five years I was at the club, I wasn't a regular in the team at all.

You would never have thought then that I would go on to play more than 550 games for the club. As I've said, my life at Oakwell, until I was 27, was made up of reserve team football and the occasional appearance in the first team.

After featuring in about half of the first team's games in my first season,

1962/63, I only played five league games in my second season with the club.

Then 23 in my third.

Twelve in my fourth.

And 14 in my fifth.

I had one or two injures, but mainly I just wasn't first choice.

Most of the time when the team sheets went up on the board, I hardly ever needed to check because I knew I would be in the reserves and not the first team.

THE END OF every season was a very nervous time.

If I got retained, I would get a letter through the door. But if a player was released, he would get called into the manager's office for a meeting. That's what we all dreaded.

April and May were awful because you were so nervous about whether you would get retained or not. Every year in those early days I thought I was going to be released because I wasn't really in the first team.

I imagined having to go back to the North East and feel like a failure; like I had been given this huge opportunity to do what I had always wanted to do but I had blown it. They were frightening times.

There were no agents in those days so there was no guarantee you would get another club if you were let go.

Every day you were just hoping that envelope would fall through the letterbox with your name on it.

Luckily for me, that happened every year.

It was a great feeling when I opened that letter.

That evening, we always went out to celebrate.

The first time I was retained, it gave me a massive boost in confidence, understanding that people at the club had faith in me. It was the manager and the coaches who made the decisions on retaining players, along with the owner.

But I still didn't play regularly for another couple of years and every time it got to the end of the season, it was a very stressful time.

In 1964 I had an offer to move to Australia and play for George Cross soccer club in Melbourne.

I was tempted because I thought I would be released by Barnsley. Myself and

Josy were making plans to move over there, in case I got released.

IN 1964, JOSY and I got married.

We had our first child, Louise the next year, so there was much more pressure on me to be retained. Suddenly I had a wife, kids and a mortgage.

We looked at houses up in County Durham in case I got released.

Another local club might have signed me, but I wanted to be prepared. I also brought my tiling tools down from Consett, in case I didn't get retained and I needed a new job. They are still in my garage now.

I actually used to keep my hand in during the summer and earn a little bit. I put a lot of roofs up on Dodworth Road, and some of them are still up now.

I replaced a solicitors' roof in Hoylandswaine and it was the only one that didn't come off when they had a big gale.

Most of us, who weren't first team regulars, took extra jobs in the summer because we went down to basic wages in those months.

I used to drive the Co-op wagon, taking goods to different shops and houses. No one really recognised me as a Barnsley player because I was in the reserves.

I also worked in a timber merchant.

I still used to go into the club during the summer just so I could kick a ball about.

A PLAYER CALLED Jimmy Sheavills was due to move into a house the club had built but he got released, and myself and Josy ended up buying that house in an area of Barnsley called Cundy Cross.

I always felt for the players who didn't get retained, because you trained with them every day and got to know them and their families very well.

I have seen some players who have been given the bad news, and I've witnessed how it can be devastating for the whole family. Sometimes, wives would go down to the club very upset, asking why this has happened to their husband.

We didn't have a carpet fitted in the new house, in case we had to move somewhere else. We knew we might have to roll it up and take it with us.

I PROBABLY HAD more of those nervous waits for an envelope than pretty much any other player. I kept getting retained, but for five long years I remained on the fringe of the first team. I never really got used to it.

There was always a fear… *Will this be the year that they finally give up on me?*

I did wonder whether I would ever make it in the first team and have a career as a footballer in the long-term. But I kept talking myself up.

If I wasn't good enough… *They would have got rid of me after a year, wouldn't they?*

That kept me going.

A lot of people would have just given in after being in the reserves so long but I don't think that way. It just made me work that bit harder to achieve my lifelong ambition of being a professional footballer.

I could easily have gone back up to the North East and become a tiler again. But I was never going to give in. I have always had a different attitude to most people.

In the end, it paid off.

« CHAPTER 4 »

WE HAD SOME good players at the club in my first few years.

Tony Leighton was an excellent goal-scorer, and one of the star players when I first arrived. His record of 64 goals in 126 games speaks for itself. He could head the ball as well as anyone I have ever seen. He was also extremely fit and very athletic.

Tony was one of those people who seemed to be good at anything he tried. He probably could have made it as a cricketer if he hadn't been a footballer. He used to play at Barnsley Cricket Club on Friday nights in a knock-out league... we all used to go down and watch him smash sixes for fun.

Tragically, Tony had Motor Neurone Disease later on. He died aged just 38 in 1978. There was a testimonial match at Huddersfield for him, which I played in. He came into the dressing-rooms in a wheelchair to try to thank us all, but he couldn't talk.

It was heart-breaking to see him like that because he had been such a fantastic athlete and a good person as well. It's so sad that that happened to him.

As well as Tony, Ken Oliver was one of the best headers of the ball in the lower divisions. He had come from South Shields a few years before me and he was well established in the Barnsley team when I arrived. He was a fantastic target man... he knew where the net was.

George Kerr was one of the players I lived with in digs. He played up front and he was quick and sharp, a natural goal scorer.

Eddie O'Hara was a smashing winger with a great left foot and a lot of pace. He was a little Scottish fella with curly hair. He could smoke for England and always wanted a fag before we went out to train. I don't know how he was so fast and so fit, considering how much he used to smoke, but he left defenders in his wake.

He was one of a group of them who used to smoke in the weight-room before training every day. As I've said once already, and may say again, it was a very different game back then.

Eddie was a good player for Barnsley, scoring and assisting goals regularly, then he moved to South Africa. He used to march about like a little gangster and always wanted us young lads to do what he told us, but he was a nice man when you got to know him.

Alan Hopper had also come from South Shields and was a very good friend of mine; still is.

He was the first-choice right-back but he always seemed to be injured when we were about to come up against a big, strong, fast winger – like Jimmy McLaughlin for instance, who played for Northern Ireland and Shrewsbury Town.

That was the joke that went around the club, that Hopper would drop out and let me play in the difficult games because I had a bit more pace than him.

'Aye up, Murph... you'll be playing again this week!' I'd hear the other players shouting at me.

I didn't mind. I was just pleased to get any opportunity.

THE CLUB HAD only just stayed in the Third Division the season before I arrived, winning 4-2 at home to Torquay United to survive on the final day in the 1961/62 campaign.

That was a familiar theme in my first few seasons as we were always quite near the bottom of the table.

My first appearance for the reserves was at Bramall Lane against Sheffield United. I played at centre-back. It was a few months after I joined, and I did quite well.

My first team debut came against Halifax Town at the Shay on September 11, 1962. I wasn't that nervous but my anxiety doubled when I realised I would be playing against a left-winger called Brian Redfearn, who must have been well over six feet.

Brian was the father of Neil Redfearn, who would become a Barnsley hero in the 1990s and take them to the Premiership.

He was one of the players Alan Hopper liked to avoid.

It wasn't easy but I played pretty well.

I had a better match a few days later, in the League Cup against Hartlepool United, and got a bit of praise in the press, which was a big confidence-booster for a young lad. We won 2-1, and I managed to make quite an important tackle right at the end to stop them equalising.

It was a big game for me. Hartlepool wasn't far away from where I had come from. I had played against some of their players for South Shields, and they were one of the clubs who had wanted to sign me.

MY HOME LEAGUE debut was a 2-1 loss to Hull City in front of 6,763 fans. The crowds that season varied from about 4,000 to as high as 10,000 for the bigger games.

One of my first away games was at Crystal Palace.

I had never been to London before so to go to a famous old ground like that was a fantastic experience. They were a big name, and I had signed professional forms for a football club to play at grounds like that. I was just so excited to be at that level of football. We won the game 2-1 as well, so it was a fantastic day.

I had been playing instead of Alan Hopper but then I picked up a slight injury and he came back.

I had a few months out of the side.

During that time, Barnsley hosted Everton in the FA Cup.

That was one of the only games the club played from November until February, as the winter of 1962/63 was known as 'The Big Freeze' across the UK.

Temperatures remained low week after week. There was a lot of snow and rain. It was terrible.

The game against Everton was cancelled four times due to the snow and ice.

As a reserves player, I was recruited to help break the ice up on the pitch and clear it so the game could go ahead. At the fourth attempt, it was eventually played, after the groundsman, Ernest Steele painted the lines a dark blue.

We lost 3-0 but it was a fantastic experience to see such quality players, like England internationals Brian Labone and Gordon West, who was from Barnsley, and to see 30,000 people at Oakwell. It was another moment when you realised you're starting to live your dream of being a footballer. Everton were a very big name at that point.

Of course, I would have preferred to have played but it just made me excited about other big nights to come.

BY THE TIME the weather improved in March, I got back in the side at left-back because Eric Brookes was injured. My role at that time was an understudy to either full-back.

We had a lot of games to make up because of all the postponements so I played my first regular first team football for Barnsley in the spring of 1963.

I gave away a penalty for hand-ball at Watford but, thankfully, they missed it and we drew 0-0.

In a home game against Colchester United, which we lost 3-2, I played against a player called John Fowler who was about five feet two and almost as wide as he was tall, but very fierce.

We went in for a challenge on the halfway line and he led with his fist and punched me in the face. He knocked me off my feet and I had to be stretchered off for the only time in my career.

There was blood everywhere from my lip and mouth.

It was in front of the old John Smith's Stand at Oakwell, as far away from the tunnel as you could get.

I would have put up with a kick, but I wasn't prepared for a punch. Fowler didn't get sent off... I don't think he even got booked. That's what it was like in those days.

I had my lip stitched back up and, being Barry Murphy, I came back out to play. There were no subs in those days. They pushed me forward into midfield but I didn't know what day it was.

The impact of the fist and the floor on my head had left me very dazed.

I lasted maybe 20 minutes and they had to take me off for good because I was seeing stars. I wanted to help the team but it didn't work.

I have heard since that John Fowler died while playing a few years after this, which is terrible.

I had a better time the next week because we won 2-0 at Hull City, which was a huge win for us because, of course, we had been battling against relegation. We secured our safety later in the month with a 1-0 victory over Reading. After that we lost 4-1 at Millwall, and I scored an own goal in a mix-up with our goalkeeper, Alan Hill.

Millwall had a reputation, as they do now, of having a fan-base with a hooligan element to it. We were told to run off the pitch as soon as possible at the final whistle.

There was nothing stopping the fans running onto the pitch at the end. There were no lines of stewards like in modern football.

The Millwall fans started to chase us as soon as the final whistle went.

Because it was the end of the season, maybe they thought they might get away with something. The back four, including myself, were the closest to them and we had to really leg it.

Fortunately, we were quicker than them, but it was pretty scary.

I will never forget that day.

We then lost 4-0 at home to Palace on the final day, in front of a crowd of only 3,738.

We finished 18th out of 24… three places and one point clear of the relegation zone.

I had packed quite a lot into my first season at Barnsley and learned a lot.

I STARTED FIVE of the first six games in the 1963/64 season but then I was out in the cold again because Alan Hopper and Eric Brookes were back in.

The match I was most disappointed to miss was an FA Cup game against Manchester United. The lads had done really well to get to the fifth round by beating Bury, Rochdale and Scunthorpe United, and they got their reward with a tie against one of the biggest clubs in the world. United were the FA Cup holders and there was a very close relationship between the two clubs as two Barnsley lads, Tommy Taylor and Mark Jones had gone to Manchester United and died in the Munich Air Disaster five years earlier.

There were 38,076 people inside Oakwell and the visiting team included

Denis Law, who scored twice, as well as Bobby Charlton and George Best.

Unfortunately, I went with the reserves to Lincoln City that day.

The secretary at the time had organised that match instead of letting us stay and watch the first team play Manchester United.

It was a terrible thing to do, and it still angers me to this day that I didn't get to see the likes of George Best in his prime at Oakwell.

All everyone in the town and the county was talking about was the best players in the world coming to Barnsley but, even though we played for the club, we couldn't watch it.

THE ONLY FIRST team game I played after September that season – which was again spent fighting relegation – was a huge one away at Brentford.

It was the penultimate game of the season. We could have been down if we had lost it. They missed a penalty late on and we drew 1-1, having come from behind. We didn't think the spot-kick should have been given against Big Eric Winstanley.

We disputed it, then burst into a round of applause when the home striker put it over the bar. I was playing as an inside-forward which was unusual for me but I was just glad to be back in the team. It made headlines before the game that Johnny Steele was going to play me, a pretty much unheard-of defender, in attack in such a massive fixture.

We still needed a point in our last game of the season against Queens Park Rangers at Loftus Road to stay up.

We were 2-0 down after 21 minutes.

It looked as if we were going down.

But Johnny Byrne pulled one back. Then Jimmy Sheavills scored a late equaliser. We survived.

AFTER THREE NARROW escapes in a row, 1964/65 would be the season when Barnsley were relegated to the Fourth Division.

We had a really tough start to the season, not winning any of our first six games, and then we suffered an embarrassing 7-0 loss at Hull City. I played against their left-winger, John McSeveney who would later be Barnsley manager. They were just too good for us that day.

I was playing most of the games early in that season and, apart from a disappointing own goal in a 1-0 loss at home to Oldham Athletic, I felt I was doing quite well in difficult circumstances.

I had been standing in for Alan Hopper at right-back, then Eric Brookes on the left, but eventually they both got back in the team and I found myself back in the reserves for a few months.

During that time out of the first team, in September, 1964, I married Josy, whom I had met the previous year.

It was a Saturday in September. I got the club's permission to get married.

None of the first team players could go because they were playing a game, but all their wives came and there are many more women than men in our wedding photos. We went on our honeymoon to Blackpool for three days because I got Monday and Tuesday off. I had borrowed a little Ford Anglia for the trip.

It was the week of the illuminations and we hadn't booked anywhere to stay. We were like Mary and Joseph trying to find somewhere.

We tried everywhere but the only place we could find was a boarding-house miles away from the seafront. We were in the attic.

It wasn't the most glamorous honeymoon and we laugh about it now, but they are happy memories.

Josy has been my career and my life. I always say that the best contract I ever signed was when I married her. She was definitely worth coming down to Barnsley for.

We have been married for 56 years and she's carried me through everything. She's been fantastic. I don't know how the heck she has put up with me for that long but I'm glad she has.

◄ ◄ ◆ ▷ ►

Josy Murphy has been married to Barry for 56 years.

BEFORE I MET Barry, I wasn't really interested in football.

I had been to a couple of games at Oakwell, because my dad was a steward on the directors' entrance, but cricket was the sport that I was more interested in.

My dad was on the selection committee at Barnsley Cricket Club and he used to umpire. I used to be the scorer for them.

Barry had met my sister, Margaret first and taken her out to the pictures.

I remember coming home one night and asking my dad where she was and he said, 'She's gone out with a footballer... but I'm sure he's married'.

He wasn't married... but he had gone out with Margaret.

Later that week she invited me to go out with her and her friends in Wakefield on a Wednesday night. She was seven years older than me and she was trying to do me a favour.

We went to the Mecca, a dance hall in Wakefield.

Barry walked in with some other players. Margaret thought he was going to ask her to dance but he walked straight past her and asked me. I didn't know who he was but I said, 'Yes' and it went from there. We were married a year later.

Margaret said later that she only went out with him because she felt sorry for him because he was living in digs.

IT WAS NERVE-WRACKING in the first few years when Barry was in the reserves because we had a young family and we never knew whether he was going to be released or not. We had been looking at houses in County Durham in case.

When it got to May and we didn't know if he had been retained, you did start to worry a bit.

But he had a trade as a tiler, which he could have gone back to, so there wasn't quite as much pressure on us as there might have been on players who couldn't do anything else.

I knew he could earn a living outside football but he wouldn't have enjoyed it as much. But eventually he got in the team and stayed in it for a long time.

His testimonial year was a highlight because there were so many occasions at working men's clubs and schools and other places. We met a lot of nice people.

I used to like going to the big clubs when they played a cup tie against Barnsley. We saw Billy Bonds' wife at West Ham. She was very glamorous.

Barry was very superstitious. He would always have to have the same food if they were on a cup run or, if they were on a good run in the league, I had to keep going to games in the same dress.

He didn't like to lose. If they did, he would be in a bad mood, just quiet and disappointed more than angry.

But he always got over it.

Being a wife of a footballer was nothing like it is now as a WAG.

It wasn't that different to being married to anyone else, because they didn't earn anywhere near the money that footballers earn now. One difference was that, if we went into town together, people used to stop him and ask him about the football. They still do that now.

The best thing about it was the time he had with the kids because he finished training at lunchtime. That meant I could train as a teacher, a job I did for 30 years.

When they were going to play Leicester City in the FA Cup, we had a family photo in the Barnsley Chronicle *with Barry putting talcum powder on our son Neil's bottom, who was a little baby. They wouldn't put that in a paper now. We still have that photo and it makes us all laugh.*

Some players spent every penny but we always saved because we knew it wouldn't last forever.

We still had some fun and we made lots of friends. When I got to be one of the older wives, I did my best to make sure that all the wives socialised and that the new arrivals were introduced to everyone.

I don't think they have as much fun now as we did back then. We made our own entertainment… we would have dinner parties at all the other players' houses.

It wasn't quite as glamorous as it is now. One of the players, John Evans got married and for their honeymoon they stayed in our bungalow in Barnsley while we went up to Durham to stay with Barry's family for a few days.

At the games, the wives were ignored. They put us on the back row of the West Stand. I just went for the gossip; we didn't really watch the match.

I used to take our son Neil and he would just run up and down the stand flicking the seats up.

There was a room with a snooker table in it for us to wait after the game, but there were no refreshments.

Allan Clarke was a lot more aware of the wives. After he arrived in 1978, he used to make sure we were treated better at games and, when the players went away in pre-

season, he would send flowers to all of the wives.

Barry was a coach by then. When he had been coaching, shouting at the players, I sometimes had to remind him that he didn't have to shout at us when he came in. He wasn't being aggressive, he just needed to turn his voice down because he had been used to shouting to the other side of the field.

He moved to Leeds and he loved it there, they were very good to us.

When he left it was a shock and probably the toughest time because he had never been unemployed.

But he got back involved with sport at Penistone Leisure Centre and scouting for other clubs.

I used to get taken to the little grounds but all his friends were taken to the big clubs.

Once he did take me to Old Trafford and I was very impressed because all the tea services on the table were silver. It was a bit different from being in the snooker room at Oakwell.

Later, when he was working for Nottingham Forest, we went to FA Cup finals and semi-finals.

Every now and then someone says to me, 'I bet you're fed up of football?' and I say, 'Well, I'm used to it by now.'

All in all, Barry has been very easy to live with and I have never been bored.

◄◄◆▷►

I GOT BACK in the first team in the spring of 1965.

We were in deep relegation trouble. To make things significantly more difficult, our top-scorer, Tony Leighton, had been sold to Huddersfield Town.

Tony had been a fantastic player for us in the previous two and a half seasons, scoring a goal every other game and playing a massive part in keeping us up. Without him, we missed a big scoring threat. We couldn't really recover.

That season we also had Martin Ferguson, the brother of Sir Alex Ferguson. He was a midfield player. He didn't play many games for us but he scored a few goals.

We still went down with two games to spare after a 1-1 draw at Oldham Athletic. The match was delayed by 20 minutes because of water on the pitch. The home team had a man sent off before half-time, but we couldn't beat them.

They took the lead, then I got the assist for the equaliser, scored by Alan Hopper who was being used as an experimental striker, but it wasn't enough.

We lost the last two games of the season at home to Workington and Mansfield, with less than 3,000 home fans at each game. We finished bottom of the league and were relegated to the Fourth Division for the first time ever.

It was humiliating for the club and a real low point. I had only played 24 league games and I wasn't very experienced, but I still felt as guilty as any other man in the club.

There was a feeling that Barnsley shouldn't be down in the Fourth Division.

It was the decade after the likes of Tommy Taylor, Danny Blanchflower and George Robledo had been playing for the club in the Second Division.

To be in the basement division was not what anyone expected.

WE WANTED TO bounce straight back.

We won our first three games of the 1965/66 Division Four season, but then inconsistency crept in and, towards the end of the campaign, we lost six matches in-a-row at the start of a 12-game winless run.

We won our last two games, 3-0 and 4-0, at home to Wrexham and Southport, so we finished 16th, three points clear of the relegation zone. If we had finished in the drop zone, we would have had to apply for re-election which would have been dreadful.

I had started the first eight matches at right-back, but then I lost my place to a new player called Bob Parker.

One thing that I remember very well from that season is that I was the club's first ever substitute.

The rules were changed in the summer of 1965 so that teams could bring players off the bench to replace someone who had an injury.

I was sitting on the bench at Luton Town on October 9.

All of a sudden, George Kerr had an injury and I had to go on. I had to get up to the pace of the game. I didn't even have a warm-up or a stretch because the concept of a substitute was all so new to us. I was just suddenly on the pitch.

We had gone 4-0 down after 19 minutes but had brought it back to 5-3 when

George had to be stretchered off. We scored again but ended up losing 5-4.

The nice thing is that it's another little bit of history. I might lose all my other records but I can never lose that one.

I was also the club's second substitute, in the 5-1 loss at home to Doncaster Rovers a few weeks later. I prefer to remember the game at Notts County when I came off the bench and set up the only goal in a 1-0 win. I was brought on as a winger and put in a cross which Bob Earnshaw converted.

Overall it was a disappointing season for the team and also for me personally. I had hoped that the one good thing about going down a level would be that there would be more opportunities for me to play.

I started nine matches that season.

I had come off the bench three times.

I wanted more.

PART TWO

Glory Years

« CHAPTER 5 »

ONCE AGAIN, I started the 1966/67 season out of the first team.

But I got back in in September and, on my second start, I managed to score my first Barnsley goal in a 2-1 win over Luton Town, which was a fantastic moment for me and a big confidence boost.

Unfortunately, I found myself out of the team for the next game and didn't play again for six months. When I did though, I made sure I stayed in the side.

On March 18, 1967, Barnsley drew 0-0 at home to Notts County at Oakwell.

It wasn't a particularly special game or one that will stick in the memory for most of the 5,347 people who were there. I can't remember that much about it except that I was picked at left-back and I had a pretty good match.

I never imagined it would be the start of a club record run of almost 200 consecutive starts which still stands to this day.

It was a run that would include a battle at the bottom of the Fourth Division in the first few months before the club nearly folded, then the only promotion of my career. And also cup games against massive top flight sides like Leicester City and Arsenal.

To play that many games in-a-row was a big achievement, especially in those days when you could kick each other without being sent off and the pitches were not good at all. It was difficult to stay fit.

It was during that run that I went from being a back-up player, who had never really had a long-term run in the team to a really established part of the side, the club and the town.

IT WAS A life-changing period of time and a spell in which I was probably at the peak of my career.

I was in my mid-to-late-twenties, so I was more mature but I was still physically at the top of my game. My legs were fresh as I hadn't played anywhere near the number of games most players my age had.

I stayed in the team until the end of that 1966/67 season, eventually moving back to right-back; then I started the next season in the side which was the promotion campaign.

I started to get really confident and I felt at home in the team. I was never going to be put back in the reserves because I was so consistent.

It was a brilliant spell for me and it made all the difficult times before seem worthwhile.

I was playing every week and performing consistently well. All of the players were close friends and we were a very good unit.

My motivation, since joining the club, had always been to get into the first team on a regular basis but then it changed to making sure I stayed in the first team… and that I didn't let my standards slip.

Everything changed from only playing now and then in front of about 2,000 supporters, to being a first-choice starter with crowds of sometimes 16,000.

It was nice getting to the end of every season and knowing for a fact that I would be retained, that a fat brown envelope would fall through the letterbox in our family home and I would have another year at my beloved Oakwell.

I was still only signing one-year contracts, because that was what every player did back then, but I knew that I was valued and would be kept on.

PEOPLE STARTED TO recognise me in the town of Barnsley.

I could walk around for the first five seasons without anyone really knowing who I was. It was an era when highlights weren't on TV and I wasn't in the local paper much so most people didn't know anything about me, until I got on that run and started getting a lot more attention.

We lived in the town, we drank in the same pubs as the fans and we shopped in the same shops.

The supporters gave me a bit of stick when things weren't going well but they weren't aggressive like some fans are now with some players.

Arthur Raynor – who became chairman of the club – had a pie shop in the Arcade and every time I walked past, if I was with my teammates or with Josy, he used to bring out a couple of pies.

There were two brothers called Barker, who had a fruit stall in the market, and when we walked past they always used to comment to us about what had happened in the last games. If you had lost, you didn't go near that stall, but it was all good-natured banter.

We had people on the board like Norman Moody, a hide and skin salesman, and various other local business people. It was very much a community club.

Once I got established, I used to do a lot of work in the community and I would be out almost every night at events and dinners. Nearly all the presentations that needed to be done, would be done by me. I would go all over the town to school events, youth clubs and social clubs.

I didn't mind doing it at all.

I made a living out of the club and the town, and the fans paid my wages, so I thought going to those events was the least I could do to repay them.

By that time, and later in my career, myself and Josy used to be the guardians of all the players and their wives. I am not sure why; maybe because I was one of the senior figures by then. They were always coming around to our house and Josy would spoil them all with food and drinks.

A lot of those players had signed from somewhere else in the country and didn't know anybody in Barnsley, especially if they were single. They needed someone to take them under their wing and I was always happy to do it. I had been at the club a long time by then and I knew what it was like to arrive and not know anyone.

WHEN I WENT back to visit my family in Crookhall, I used to feel like a million dollars because everyone knew who I was.

They always looked out for Barnsley's results.

I used to love going back because I felt like a bit of a hero or celebrity.

I wasn't playing at the top level but I had still made it as a professional footballer, which was very unusual for someone from the tiny village of Crookhall.

I was asked to open new community centres and do presentations and I would get mentions in the local paper.

The first time I took Josy there was New Year's Eve. When you had a drink in one house, you had to go to the next house; they would be insulted if you didn't. Josy bailed out at about 2am and I was out until 5am.

Later, when we went up there as a family, the kids used to be amazed by the attention I got but my mother used to bring me back down to earth.

'You think your dad's Georgie Best... but he's not!' she'd tell them.

My brother, Brian hardly ever missed a game that I played in. He travelled from the North East across the country to watch me. The supporters used to know him better than they knew me. My mother would come down as well sometimes.

I WAS KNOWN as a player who put himself about a lot on the pitch.

I used to look at my opponent and think... *It's either his mortgage that's due... or mine.*

I always gave as good as I got.

I was very tough-tackling and I used to hope for a ball that was slightly closer to me than the winger in the first few minutes of the match so I could slide in, win it and clatter him – then I was in the game and I felt like I had started to get into his head.

I probably wouldn't have lasted 90 minutes if I played like that in this modern era but I like to think I would have been able to discipline myself.

I can't stand the diving I see in the game these days and, if they did that in my day, they wouldn't have got back up. I was a natural defender and I sensed danger. I saved quite a few shots off the line.

I headed three shots off the line in an FA Cup game in Darlington and got a headline in the *Sunday People* which claimed, *"Murphy is Oakwell's saviour"*. Brian was in the stands with the Darlington fans and he said they were all talking about me and giving me a bit of praise.

THE CROWD AT Oakwell used to shout at me quite a lot.

As a full-back, I used to play next to the side of the pitch so I could hear what they were all saying, especially when I was taking a throw-in.

But it was all good-natured banter.

I think the Barnsley fans took to me basically straight away because I was hard-working and consistent. That gave me a lot of confidence and I didn't want to let them down. I always got on very well with the fans and, because they paid my wages, I used to see them as the most important people

I always felt nervous before every game I played. I never went out full of confidence because that could trip you up. I was just hoping that I would have a good game and, if I did and we won, the beer tasted like champagne.

If we lost, the kids would be in bed early and Josy used to say it was a good job we didn't have a dog because I would kick it. She was joking, but I could get into a foul mood. I didn't used to speak to anyone for a while after we lost because it used to really hurt me.

I just wanted to do well in everything I ever did and I used to always say, 'Nothing for losers'.

I once scored an own goal in a game we lost 1-0.

I made Josy stay at the ground with me until I knew the bus station was empty and no fans would be there.

I HAVE ALWAYS been very superstitious.

I had to put my shorts on last and be last out of the dressing-room before a game, unless I was captain then I was first out. If we won a game, Josy had to wear the same outfit to the next one.

I always had egg and sherry the night before every game. It's just egg and milk mixed together with a spoonful of sherry and some sugar. My mother used to make it for me when I was a kid in the North East, to build me up.

Then it became a tradition to have it before every game.

I used to have a walk every night before a match, just half a mile up the road.

When I was defending a corner kick, I used to kick the base of the post with both feet.

It probably all started when something went right and I just kept doing it. I never used to forget any of the superstitions.

A lot of people in football, I suppose, are very superstitious.

When I was a coach under Allan Clarke, one Easter weekend we had a good result in the first game and we wanted to wear exactly the same kit for the Monday match but the laundry wasn't open at the club.

So Josy washed all of our kits and dried them on the washing line in our back garden. It must have been a strange sight for the neighbours, to see all these Barnsley FC shirts, shorts and socks hanging on our line.

I WAS GIVEN the nickname of Spud quite early in my Barnsley career.

They used to shout it from the terraces and I was called *"Spud Murphy"* in some newspaper headlines as well.

No one had called me that in the North East.

Some of the older Barnsley fans call me that name still, when they see me out and about in town. I don't like it, I prefer to be called Barry… because that's my name. But it doesn't matter; it was always affectionate.

Josy says it's because potatoes are called Murphy in Ireland, but we don't really know why I got the nickname.

I CAN PICTURE all the goals I scored, which isn't that difficult because there were only three.

The first one was against Luton Town in September, 1966.

Johnny Steele played me up front because of injuries to other players and I got a tap-in from a cross by Dick Hewitt to open the scoring in a 2-1 win. I was under the bar and anyone could have scored it but it was a massive relief and confidence boost to get my first professional goal.

I had to wait for my next goal until August, 1969, in a 3-3 draw at Bristol Rovers. I was captain that day, because Big Eric didn't play. John Evans had the ball on the left wing and I must have got a nose-bleed because I sprinted up from right-back into the box. The goalkeeper saved my header but I kicked in the rebound from a few yards out.

It was a big stadium and I ran around it in celebration. Rovers went 2-1 up soon after, then they went 3-2 ahead but we came back to draw.

That Eastville Stadium has been knocked down now, which is a shame because it was a real collector's item – one of only three grounds where I scored a goal.

I then had to wait eight years – and hundreds of games – for my third goal, and my only one ever at Oakwell. It was a penalty in a 4-0 home win over Rochdale, the first game of the 1977/78 season that proved to be my last campaign as a player.

We used to practice penalties every day after training and that season, I was the one who scored the most – maybe because I had been doing it so long.

I just used to put my head down and hit it as hard as I could. That's what I did in the match, after Peter Price was fouled, and it went in to make it 2-0 after less than 20 minutes.

I missed a penalty a few weeks later against Newport County and people still mention that to me. I went with the same technique of going for pure power, but it hit the bar and went all the way out of the penalty area. We won that game anyway but four goals would have been better than three.

Having said that, three is better than none and I'm glad I got to experience the feeling of scoring a goal for the club I loved.

Full-backs didn't get forward much at all in those days, not like in modern football.

The centre-halves went up the pitch so they would score.

I didn't score many but I stopped a lot. That was more satisfying to me than scoring, but I enjoyed both.

TOWARDS THE END of the 1966/67 season, the club was in big trouble on and off the pitch.

There was a bit of chaos behind the scenes and the financial situation was very difficult.

We were bottom of the Football League briefly for the first time in our history, playing in front of crowds of slightly more than 2,000, and running out of money to keep the business going.

Everybody thought the club was going to fold and it got very, very close. The news cameras were rolling as we were training, because everyone thought it might be our last training session. That happened a few times.

There weren't many times that we made it onto the news in those days but, unfortunately, that was one of them.

It was awful and you could sense around the town that everyone was very worried. It affected everybody who worked at the club and relied on the club for their livelihood, from the players all the way down to the washing ladies in the laundry.

It got to the point where we couldn't really train properly because we only had one ball which we needed for the league games; so we used to just run all day.

They stopped us having pre-match meals. Instead, we used to stop at a motorway services and the manager, Johnny Steele would give every player a pound to get a cup of tea and a sandwich.

Eventually, the club was saved.

Some of the big businessmen in the town got together and paid the wages. Ernest Dennis and Geoffrey Buckle joined the board as directors and raised £10,000 to steady the ship. Everybody was so relieved and the club really kicked on from that point. The new investors also provided the money for Johnny Steele to sign important players, like Barrie Thomas and John Evans.

But there was more bad news to come.

The long-serving chairman, Joe Richards, who had been on the board since 1919 and chairman for 21 years, had stepped down and was replaced by Sid Edmundson, who put some money into the club.

Sid always used to go for a walk in Locke Park before every game and, one day, when we were going to York City, he collapsed and died in the park. He was found dead on a bench. It was only four days after he had been made chairman.

That was a motivator for the team and, along with the new signings and a bit more financial security, things improved on the pitch.

Arthur Raynor, another local businessman, took over as chairman.

Eventually we got a couple of big wins and finished four points above the bottom four, so we didn't need to seek re-election.

THE 1967/68 SEASON, in which we got promoted from the Fourth Division, was a special one, and a huge turnaround from the battles against relegation and financial collapse just a few months before.

It was the first and only time I got promoted in my playing career.

It has to be my favourite season but really, I just loved playing football for all those years and a promotion was the icing on the cake.

As a team, we worked extremely hard. We had trained throughout pre-season in some woods in Pogmoor. We ran so much in those woods that we knew what time the trains would be coming by on the tracks nearby.

The success was built on our defence, with myself at right-back, Pat Howard and Eric Winstanley at centre-back and Eric Brookes at left-back.

All of the other three were from Barnsley and I was the only 'outsider', so to speak. But we were very close as friends off the pitch and that helped us in games. Myself and Pat played every match that season. If Eric Brookes was injured, I would move onto the left of the defence and Bob Parker would play at right-back.

You hear about defences like Arsenal in the 1980s and 90s under George Graham, who were so well-drilled, and we were a bit like that but at a lower level.

Norman Rimmington and Johnny Steele used to drill us every day individually, and as a back four. We knew everything about each other, all of our strengths and weaknesses.

We worked very, very hard on our defending and playing as a unit, and it showed in matches.

PEOPLE OFTEN ASK me who was the best player I played with and I always say Eric Winstanley.

He was the perfect all-round centre-back – tall, good on the ball and good in the air. He would keep attackers quiet and be a threat at the other end from set-pieces.

If he hadn't badly injured his knee ligaments in his early twenties, I honestly believe he would have played for England.

He had played for the national team at youth level and I really think he could have gone all the way to the top if he had stayed fit. Clubs like Manchester United and Tottenham Hotspur were chasing him but he never quite got back to that level after the injury, although he was still an incredible performer for us.

Me and Eric were big mates, from as soon as I came down to Barnsley. He more or less took me under his wing, even though he was four years younger than me. He had come through the youth system at Barnsley, which was his hometown club.

We went everywhere together.

His family lived on Lindhurst Road in Athersley and I used to go there every Friday for fish and chips. That helped me a lot, because I was moving to a new area and it was great to have a good pal who knew the town and the club.

Eric wasn't the best of trainers, however. He used to have a go at me because I would always be way out in front when we were running. But in games he was magnificent for Barnsley.

Eric was also a massive threat when he went forward.

He scored 14 goals in the 1968/69 season.

Eventually, Jim Iley sold him to Chesterfield, which wasn't really an improvement for him. It was sad to see Eric leave because he was a fantastic player and very popular with the fans.

I took over from him as the Barnsley player to have made the most appearances.

He was definitely a better player than I was but I just managed to hang around a bit longer. If he had stayed, he would certainly have put that record well out of my reach.

ALONGSIDE ERIC WAS Pat Howard.

They were a terrific partnership at centre-back. Third and Fourth Division attacks just couldn't get through them. Eric was always the first man to tackle or head the ball, then Pat would be there to sweep up afterwards.

I think Eric was the more talented player but it was Pat who eventually got to the highest level, playing for Newcastle United and then Arsenal.

Pat, who was from Dodworth in Barnsley, was a proper defender and hard as nails. He came into the first team at 18 years-old and you could tell he was going to make it to the top. As well as being a very good defender, he would smash in some wonderful free-kicks at the other end.

THE BACK FOUR was completed by Eric Brookes, who was one of the players I looked up to when I first joined the club.

He was a left full-back and a smashing player. He came through from the intermediate team and was already in the first team by the time I arrived.

Eric was a local lad and played for an England youth team. He was 16 years-old when he got into the Barnsley first team.

He lived next door to me for a while on Robert Avenue in Cundy Cross. I got on very, very well with him. When he left the club, having played more than 300 games, I never thought I would get anywhere near that many appearances for Barnsley.

Our careers were the opposite to each other because he started off so early, then left when he was 25, whereas I was a late starter and carried on until I was nearly 40. But he was an inspiration to me as a long-serving player who was fantastic for the club.

I was very sad when Eric died early in 2020. He was a wonderful man.

I CAN REEL off the rest of that promotion team very easily.

Our goalkeeper was Roy Ironside. He was a massive guy but a gentle giant and a very good keeper. He used to give us a lot of confidence because he would claim all the crosses and communicate very well with us.

John Bettany and Dick Hewitt were our lions in the middle of the park.

Barnsley fans talk about Neil Redfearn and Ronnie Glavin as the best midfielders the club has ever had, and I understand that. But I wish more of them had seen John Bettany play. He was a fantastic footballer.

We called him a little genius because he was something special. He could find passes or make runs that no one else could. He didn't miss many games but, when he did, there was a big difference in our team.

John and Dick were the engine room of our team. Dick was more of a runner and a worker but they complemented each other very well. They both had pace and they kept our team ticking all game.

Jimmy Robson came in from Burnley and he was fantastic, a very educated footballer who had played at a higher level. He made his debut at Chesterfield in the FA Cup and they hadn't lost a game in two seasons. We beat them 3-2 and Jimmy had an excellent game, dictating play from the middle of the park.

Jimmy was a very likeable guy and extremely polite. He used to come to our house for his lunch when he first arrived and, for the first two weeks, he was too polite to tell Josy that he didn't like milk in his tea. Jimmy was my room-mate when we were on away trips and was a very good friend.

Our wingers were George Hamstead on the left, and Bob Earnshaw on the right. Bob was a PE schoolteacher in Rotherham and only part-time with us. He was extremely fast and frightened defenders. George didn't have that pace but he had more ability, with a really good left foot.

They both put a lot of crosses into the box and provided a lot of assists.

THE THING THAT pushed us on to success was the quality the club had added up front in John Evans and Barrie Thomas who scored most of the goals. Evans was born and bred in Liverpool but had been playing down at Exeter City and he was desperate to get back up to the north.

He told Johnny Steele that he was four years younger than he actually was. He said he was 24, when he was actually 28.

John really wanted the move and he didn't think Steele would sign him if he knew his actual age. This was before you could just go on to the internet and check any player's age and everything else about them.

You wouldn't get away with it now.

This all came out years later, but it didn't really matter because he had scored a lot of goals and been a fantastic player for us. If he hadn't lied, he might never have signed and I might never have got the only promotion of my career.

I have another story about John Evans.

He had broken his leg and he asked me to drive him to his family's home in Liverpool. He had a little sports car, which was quite flash and expensive for the time, and I drove him across in it.

His family lived at the top of a block of flats in a working-class area. We left the car outside and, by the time we got upstairs, there were gangs of kids sitting inside it and on it. We were shouting for them to get off it and I had to run back down the stairs.

It was one of those bizarre moments that sticks in your mind. Even in those days, before the money went stratospheric in football in the 1990s, there was a big gap in the lifestyle of footballers and the people in the places they came from.

On the pitch, John Evans was a fantastic player and a regular goal-scorer.

Barrie Thomas used to take all the work off John. He was a stocky guy who held the ball up really well. They worked perfectly together up front and fired us to promotion.

Roger Barton and John Hobson were the back-up forwards; then we had Allen Bradbury, who chipped in with a lot of goals in the promotion run-in.

It really was a fantastic team. We all knew our jobs and we had a lot of team spirit and togetherness.

WHEN I HAD arrived at Barnsley, we were getting crowds of less than 3,000, which was smaller than at South Shields, and I felt like I could look into the stand and know everybody's name.

But, by the end of the promotion season, we were averaging 15,000 crowds and the place was buzzing more than I have ever known it in my playing career.

We won our first game of the season at home against Doncaster Rovers, who were our big local rivals in those days, but then didn't win any of our next five.

But something felt a bit different to me that season; I don't know whether it was because I was in the team regularly or because we had had a very good pre-season on the training pitch, but it felt as though something good was going to happen.

We went through the entire season unbeaten at home, something Barnsley wouldn't do again until the 2018/19 campaign more than half a century later. We won 17 and drew six of our 23 home games as teams found Oakwell a very, very difficult place to go to. The confidence was oozing out of each and every one of us and we never even considered that we could lose.

We had a few scares, like a 2-2 draw with Wrexham on a Tuesday night in March when I cleared two off the line and we didn't play well, but generally we were excellent in front of our fans at Oakwell.

Away from home, we had some more difficult games like a 4-1 loss at Southend United and a 3-3 draw at Crewe Alexandra, after we were 3-1 up. I conceded a very harsh penalty as they came back to get a point.

But we had some good trips as well, like a 2-1 win just before Christmas at Doncaster Rovers, where I again saved a couple off the line and we really had to battle for a point. And a 3-2 January win at Chesterfield when Big Eric, our leader at the back, was suspended. It was great to go to all these different clubs as a side competing for promotion and with a lot of fans behind us.

Ourselves and Luton were at the top of the table for pretty much the whole season. It was a fantastic battle and we used to always look at the table to see who was on top after each game. In those days, we had to wait until the newspapers came out to see other results and the table, because we couldn't just check our mobile phones in the dressing-room like they do now.

In March, we were in the promotion places and there was a lot of pressure on us but Johnny Steele took us all away for a week to Lilleshall National Sports Centre in Shropshire. It was a good move; it let us clear our heads and just get a little bit of distance from the town of Barnsley, where there was so much expectation on us. That was Norman Rimmington's idea because he used to go down to Lilleshall a lot to get his qualifications.

At the start of April we lost 1-0 at Bradford City, who scored in the last minute, but that seemed to spur us on as we won our next five games including a 4-1 victory at Notts County.

We then went to Chester for our last away game, needing a point to go up, with one more home game remaining after that trip.

Big Eric headed us in front and that settled our nerves.

Eddie Loyden, who would sign for us later in the year, equalised for Chester but the match finished 1-1.

We were up.

AFTER THE GAME, we all went up on the balcony at Chester's Sealand Road stadium where the directors were.

I went up without my shorts on because I had taken them off in the dressing-room and didn't have a chance to put them back on. I was chased up into the directors' box in just my pants. I got ridiculed for that for years to come but I didn't mind because it was a wonderful day to look back on.

We didn't get back home until 4am because we were stopping at different pubs all the way back to drink with supporters and celebrate.

It was a fantastic night, one of the best of my life.

I always used to go to a pub in Hoyle Mill, in Barnsley, with some of our neighbours and the first time I walked in after promotion they were all waiting for me and they put *Congratulations* by Cliff Richard on the jukebox as loud as possible.

We played Newport County in our last game of the season and, after the final whistle, to see all the fans run onto the pitch to celebrate with us was fantastic.

The stands were nearly empty.

It was a marvellous feeling. I sometimes look at the photographs of me being mobbed by the crowd and it brings it all back. We had a police escort to get off the pitch. The fans didn't mean any harm, they just wanted to celebrate with us.

The club held a promotion dinner at Keresforth Hall with a lot of businessmen, people from the council and fans. It was fantastic to see what it meant to the community of Barnsley. Josy was there in a maternity dress because she was eight and a half months pregnant with our son, Neil.

That was a great year... a baby and a promotion.

I think that season was a real saviour for the club, coming so soon after all that financial trouble. To think that, just one year before, the club had nearly folded, and now we were promoted. It made it even sweeter.

Things could have gone another way if we hadn't done so well on the pitch and attracted fans back to the club. It set up a lot of the success which was still to come.

◂ ◂ ◆ ▸ ▸

Pat Howard was the youngest member of the back four that helped earn Barnsley promotion in 1967/68, and an ever-present that season along with Barry. He eventually played in the First Division with Newcastle United and Arsenal.

BARRY MURPHY WAS one of the greatest helps to my career that I could ever have wished for.

When I first started playing for the Barnsley reserves, he was very, very encouraging to me and the other young lads in that team.

Week in, week out, we were playing against the second teams of Manchester United and Everton and other big clubs, and they had some very good players.

It was very tough for the likes of me because I was only a kid. I was 15 when I started playing for the reserves – a skinny lad of about 10 stone and five feet eight tall – and we were playing in big stadiums against international players.

Most of our reserves players were very young, because the club didn't have a lot of money and didn't have a lot of players. So, to have someone like Barry, who had a bit of first team experience and was a bit older, was invaluable.

I remember Barry having an argument with a couple of the attacking players on the bus back from a reserves game. They were complaining, so he was telling them they needed to start scoring goals before they criticised anybody else.

That was the way he would express himself because he was the older player in the reserves and he didn't like the young players being too cocky. He was a leader and an authority figure, and eventually he took that into the first team as well.

I will always be grateful for Barry's enthusiasm and encouragement; he definitely helped me get to the First Division. I will never be able to thank him enough. It was a pleasure to have known him.

He was a good player, a good talker and a very good defender. I looked up to him a lot.

We both got in the first team at more or less the same time and the promotion season in 1967/68 definitely stands out. It was very tight between us and Luton Town, and the nerves came in a lot towards the end.

The most enjoyable thing was to see the crowds growing every week because of the results we were getting. All my family were coming to the games and they were really happy that I was in the team.

For the last few games, we were playing in front of 15,000, then they all ran onto the pitch after the last match of the season. That was my best day as a Barnsley player.

We had got promotion the game before when we drew at Chester, but we nearly lost because Eddie Loyden – who would go on to play for Barnsley – hit the bar with a shot from about 30 yards. I thought it was in and it would have been a very nervous last game if it had hit the back of the net.

Barry and I played on the same side of the defence and we would always cover for each other. We were a good pair.

Then we had one of the best players Barnsley has ever had in Eric Winstanley alongside us.

I am sure Eric would have gone to the highest level if he hadn't suffered a bad injury. He was one of the best players I have ever played with or against, even in the First Division. It is such a shame that he hurt his knee because it affected him very badly and he was never quite the same. But he was a great captain and a great teammate.

With Eric Brookes as well, it was a decent back four for any level in any era.

Barry and Big Winnie had a great sense of humour and they always got us laughing in the dressing-room.

Johnny Steele and Norman Rimmington were very good coaches to work for. You could always have a good conversation with Norman, he would have a word in your ear and develop you as a player. He was always laughing and joking and he had a very dry and witty sense of humour.

Johnny Steele would leave a lot of the training to Norman but, on matchdays, the boss would motivate us all and he was very firm. He wasn't someone you would ever argue with but he had a very good management style.

It was a lovely era to play for Barnsley and it was a great upbringing for me as a footballer.

I had been offered a trial by Sheffield United when I was 15. They were in the top flight at the time. But I thought I would play it safe and sign for my hometown club. I had come through the Barnsley Boys team and I used to watch them as a little boy.

They were always the team that I had wanted to play for. It proved a very good choice to start at the lower level and get experience before moving on.

I had a few good seasons under my belt and other clubs started to look at me.

I played in a behind-closed-doors practice match for Barnsley against Derby County and Brian Clough told me years later that he had organised it to look at myself, Stewart Barrowclough and Eric Winstanley.

Nobody told us at the time why we were playing this game, but Cloughie told me later. He said he tried to sign me but Barnsley were asking for too much money and he decided instead to sign Colin Todd, who went on to play for England.

A bit later, I asked Johnny Steele for a pay rise.

He had just moved to a new role at the club as general manager, after John McSeveney came in as manager. Johnny said I couldn't have any more money so I told him I wanted to leave. We had a falling out and he called me arrogant.

'Who do you think you are?' he said to me.

A few weeks later I was doing some gardening and my wife, Rita came out to tell me, 'Johnny Steele is at the front door'.

I thought she was joking but he was really there. He told me to come down to the club looking smart for 2pm that day.

I got down to Oakwell and there were hardly any cars in the car-park apart from *one very nice one with a sticker on it from a garage in Gateshead.*

So, I thought... Are they shipping me off to Gateshead?

They were a non-league side at the time.

But I walked in and Joe Harvey, the Newcastle United manager, was there. He told me he wanted me to sign for them, which I did.

Barry and all his family were Newcastle-mad so I think, although he was happy for me, he probably wished he could go up and play for them as well. He got into the Barnsley team at a later age than me which is a pity because he was a good player and could have held his own against anybody.

One of the reasons I left at the time was because the club needed to cash in.

It hadn't been that long since Barnsley FC nearly folded and they had to get all the money for players that they could, to help the club stay afloat.

Barnsley got relegated that season, in 1971/72, which was very sad to see from afar.

I got straight in Newcastle's first team and had a great five years up there, captaining them and playing in the FA Cup final, the League Cup final and winning the Anglo-Italian Cup.

I went on to play for Arsenal, Birmingham and Bury and I live in that area now.

As for Barry, he stayed at Oakwell for the rest of his playing career, as everyone knows.

He was a credit to the club on the pitch and he still is now off the pitch.

He was very, very professional.

You don't play nearly 600 games for one club without being a special person. I don't think anybody will ever break that Barnsley record. He gave absolutely everything to the club. You don't get many players with his calibre and personality.

He is 'Mr Barnsley'.

« CHAPTER 6 »

WE WERE BACK in the Third Division for the 1968/69 season.

It was a step up in quality, not a huge one, but you could definitely tell we had gone to another level.

We were delighted to be in the third tier and the fans were coming to support us in bigger numbers; like 16,000 for some games.

Johnny Steele didn't really make many new signings but we kept the majority of the promotion team together. A few new players came in like Norman Dean; a good goal scorer who arrived from Cardiff City and lived in Hemsworth. Mrs Dennis, the chairman's wife, was on a local adoption committee and she helped Norman and his wife adopt a child. It was that kind of community club at the time.

We still had the same solid back four – one of the best in the division – and we were just a very good unit from front to back.

We came tenth in our first season in the Third Division, which we were fairly happy with.

ON A PERSONAL note, that season I captained the team for the first time when Eric Winstanley was injured.

It was a massive personal honour for me and just another sign that I was really becoming a big part of the club.

We had a difficult start to the season, not winning any of our first seven games including a 5-1 thrashing at Luton Town, who had just come up with us.

Unfortunately, our unbeaten home run, which lasted all through the previous season, ended in the first match when we lost 3-2 at home to Barrow.

People in the press and some of the fans were questioning whether we were good enough for the Third Division and suggesting we would go straight back down. The turning point for us seemed to be when we played Millwall in the League Cup.

They were in the division above us at the time and were massive favourites to beat us. We drew the first game 1-1 at Oakwell and then did the same at The Den, before losing 3-1 after extra-time. We played some really good football over the two games however and, by the end of the second game, the Millwall fans were chanting 'BARNSLEY... BARNSLEY' and booing their own players.

We were disappointed to lose but we got a big boost from how well we had done against a team in the league above us, and we took that into our Third Division form.

We soon got off the mark with a win over Southport, as we came from 1-0 down with 20 minutes to go, thanks to goals by Eric Winstanley and Jimmy Robson. In our next home game, we thrashed Brighton and Hove Albion 4-0; then beat our old adversaries Luton 3-1, avenging the 5-1 loss earlier in the season.

Suddenly we were on another excellent home run and 13 league games at Oakwell over six months brought us eight wins and five draws. But our away form was much worse and we only won three on our travels all season in the league.

If we had been a bit better on the road, we might have been in contention for another promotion.

The away wins were sweet though, like when Watford scored after 12 seconds but we came back to win 2-1, with Eric equalising before Robson turned in one of my crosses for the winner.

We also won 4-1 at Crewe in January, with Eddie Loyden scoring twice – and 1-0 at Barrow, despite having Big Eric sent off with 25 minutes left after a scuffle with a former Barnsley player, Roy McCarthy.

It was another season when we had a lot of games called off in winter and had a backlog in March and April with 17 fixtures in 60 days.

A run of eight without a win started to drag us back down towards the relegation zone but we won the last five home matches. One of those was a memorable game against Watford who only needed a point to win the title.

Their fans were chanting… 'WE ARE THE CHAMPIONS' at 2-0 up but Eric scored a hat-trick and we won 3-2. Eric really was an unstoppable player in attack and defence when he was at his best, and he scored 14 goals from centre-back that season.

That season also saw us play a midweek friendly against a team from Czechoslovakia, Prague Bohemians. They had some famous names like Antonin Panenka.

We beat them 3-1, which was a great result for us.

THE 1968/69 CAMPAIGN also brought the only time I played on TV.

It was a 2-2 draw at home to Tranmere Rovers on March 29, 1969, shown on ITV with Barry Davies commentating. It also brought a buzz to Oakwell… there were cameras on top of the concrete dugouts.

It wasn't a great game because the wind was very, very strong and a lot of crosses into the box caused chaos.

Being on TV didn't really change our mindset. We just played as we normally played. The banter was funny before the game because we were all saying, 'Make sure you get your teeth cleaned!'

And… 'Make sure your boots are polished!'

It was also my 150th appearance for the club.

There was an own goal from either side and our goalkeeper, Roy Ironside let the ball go through his legs. It was probably the only game he ever played on TV and he made a big mistake in it.

He hardly ever made mistakes so he was very unlucky. I felt sorry for him.

WE CAME SEVENTH in 1969/70 – only three points off third – having been high up in the table before Christmas but then falling away a little bit.

We had been hoping for another promotion into the Second Division, which would have been fantastic for the club, but it was all about finances. The board didn't spend that extra bit of money to get the quality we needed to get us another promotion.

One or two more players of that Second Division quality probably would have got us there.

But, after the financial oblivion we had just faced, you couldn't blame the directors for not splashing more cash and taking risks. They were all putting their own money in, which they had worked hard for.

They only had so much and were doing their best for the club.

A lot of good players from the promotion season had left that summer, including Roy Ironside, Eric Brookes, Dick Hewitt, John Hobson, Roger Barton and Bob Parker.

One of our first games was a League Cup loss to Halifax at Oakwell. After the game our manager, Johnny Steele had a fight in the tunnel with the Halifax manager, Alan Ball Senior. It was a right barney.

They hated each other.

Halifax had to come back to Oakwell a few months later for a league game and there was a police investigation because Alan Ball had been sent a letter threatening him with a bullet laced with cyanide if he turned up. There were extra police. And he sat in the stand instead of the dugout, but nothing happened.

For some reason, maybe because the clubs were close to each other, there was always needle in those games against Halifax and they were always a big battle.

We had a wonderful start to the league season, winning nine of our first 13 matches and only losing two by late November. We were riding high in the top places in the division which meant we were getting bonuses in our pay but, more importantly, the fans and players were starting to dream of the Second Division.

There were some thrilling games early on, like a 3-3 draw at Bristol Rovers, in which I got my second goal for the club, and a 4-3 win at home to Reading.

It was that season that I played against my toughest ever opponent, Fulham's flying winger Les Barrett. He was a nightmare to defend against, with his pace and power, but I think I did a decent job against him as we drew 0-0 at Craven Cottage.

I was on decent form at the time and cleared three off the line in a 0-0 draw at Darlington in the FA Cup.

That was also the game which probably brought me personally the most headlines of any game in my career, because the FA Cup was a big deal in those days and a lot of local and national papers covered the tie at Darlington.

There wasn't much else to report apart from my clearances!

It was during a club record nine-match unbeaten run away from home.

I MISSED MY first football match in almost three years in December, 1969 when I had to come off at half-time in a 3-3 draw at home to Bury, but I was back in the starting line-up again for the next match. I was relieved because I didn't want to lose my long record of starting games or, more importantly, my place in the team.

We won 2-1 in a local derby at home to Doncaster Rovers just after Christmas in front of 17,186, which was a huge crowd in those days. That result ended a run of one win in 11, then we began the 1970s with a 5-1 thrashing of Gillingham at Oakwell.

By February we were unbeaten in five and could have gone joint top of the Third Division but we lost at home to Plymouth Argyle. That was the first of three successive losses which left us well off the promotion places and we could never quite recover, despite a strong end to the season.

On a personal note, in April, 1970, I passed the previous record of 164 consecutive games held by Harry Hough, a goalkeeper from the 1940s and 50s. I equalled the record in a 6-2 loss at Reading but the game in which I broke the record was a much happier occasion because we won 3-0 at home to Torquay United.

I kicked two off the line and managed to set up the opening goal for a 17 year-old called Kenny Brown.

EVENTUALLY I WAS dropped on Halloween night in 1970 at home to Doncaster Rovers, after being in the team for more than three years and 182 consecutive matches.

I was sitting in the dressing-room before the game and, suddenly, I could see people looking at the team sheet, which had just gone up on the wall… and muttering while glancing over at me.

I went over and my name wasn't on it.

I was told I had been dropped.

I hadn't been used to having setbacks for a few years so it hit me pretty hard.

I know football is a team game but I had worked so hard to keep myself fit and consistent across five years to stay in the team and help the club.

I felt sick.

I wasn't expecting it at all. I was down and out, sitting on the bench and feeling sorry for myself.

Lawrie McMenemy, my old friend from the North East, was the Doncaster manager at that time. He walked into his dugout and saw me sitting on the substitutes bench when the game was about to start.

'I'm glad you're sitting in there, Murph,' he told me, '… and you're not out on that pitch.' It was nice to hear, but it didn't really make me feel any better.

We had a difficult start to the 1970/71 season and were languishing near the bottom of the table.

I had been going through a poor patch of form, in truth, and Johnny Steele dropped me for a lad called Paul Turner, who was a teenager from Barnsley.

The manager told me he wanted to have a look at Paul. With me not getting any younger, he wanted to have a back-up.

It was his decision to make as the manager.

He wanted to give me a kick up the backside, into the bargain.

I didn't have any animosity towards him about that.

I had to remind myself that I was just grateful to be a professional footballer.

It backfired on Johnny because Paul didn't do so well and I managed to get back into the team for the next game, in the Sheffield Cup against Sheffield United, and I set up two goals in a 3-2 win.

I also started in the league the following Saturday and began another long run. I was determined not to lose my place again so I worked on my game a lot and I was more attacking that season, setting up a few goals and plenty of chances for my teammates.

It was worse for some players that season.

Billy Brindle had signed from Everton. He lived next door to us. He didn't play much and his wife went down to the club to complain. He didn't last long after that.

The game I had missed was part of a five-match losing run in the league which had us in a bit of trouble but we won the next four in the league, and pretty much stayed away from relegation danger for the rest of the season, eventually finishing 12th. We tightened up a lot defensively and kept five clean sheets in-a-row towards the end of the season.

Some of the old stalwarts had left us, like John Bettany and Jimmy Robson, but we had decent youngsters coming through such as Kenny Brown. The defence was nearly the same with myself, Eric and Pat Howard, but the rest of the team were all different from the 1967/68 promotion side.

We struggled to score regular goals for a lot of the season because John Evans was out injured and we didn't have a ready-made replacement.

AS WELL AS our journey from the Fourth Division to competing to be in the Second Division, we had some good cup runs in the late 1960s and early 70s.

We played Leicester City in the FA Cup third round in January, 1969, and they were a big team at the time.

We had won replays against Darlington and Rochdale to get to that stage, sneaking through after drawing both of the first games 0-0. The football hadn't been great but we battled hard and felt we had earned a plum tie against Leicester.

We were really geared up for it as a team and there were 25,099 people at Oakwell which was incredible to see – especially since, when I started, it was only two or three thousand.

Leicester had a very high quality team – Peter Shilton was their goalkeeper and they had seven internationals in total.

Allan Clarke, who would go on to be Barnsley manager and have a huge influence on my later career, was playing up front for the Foxes. We drew with them 1-1 at Oakwell which was a fantastic result for a Third Division side.

They took the lead midway through the first half, then Johnny Evans equalised for us. We had chances to win and it was a very good atmosphere at Oakwell with the fans really getting behind us.

Then we went down to Filbert Street in front of 31,000 and gave as good as we got again.

They took the lead with a very controversial goal by Rodney Fern, which we all thought was offside.

I had been tackled from behind a few minutes earlier and Norman Rimmington had given me some treatment at the side of the pitch. He was still walking round when Leicester scored, so was in the perfect position to see it was offside.

He was going mad on the touchline and he mentioned it regularly until his dying day. It is one of those days which plays on your mind because you feel a bit robbed.

The referee was Jack Taylor, who was the top English official at the time and would go on to referee the 1974 World Cup final.

He did give us a penalty which was scored by Eddie Loyden but Leicester got the winner.

I worked with Allan Clarke a lot later, but I never really wanted to bring that offside goal up with him.

Leicester would get to the final that year, losing to Manchester City, so to nearly beat them showed what we could do as a team. We more than matched them over the two games and it showed how good a side we were.

IN 1971, IN the League Cup, we played Arsenal at Highbury

We lost 1-0 against a side with Bob Wilson, Frank McLintock and Pat Rice in it.

It was another fantastic experience. That was exactly what I wanted to be doing when I was working hard as a young kid to become a professional footballer.

It wasn't always glamour in the cups for us, however, because we lost to Welsh non-league club, Rhyl in the FA Cup in 1970.

The first match, in Wales, was a typical cup tie when a non-league team plays against a professional side. It was on a slope, in bad weather and a very physical game. We took a fair few fans and played them off the park but we couldn't get the winner and drew 1-1.

We took them back to Oakwell and we still couldn't beat them.

We drew 0-0 and so we had to play a third game at a neutral ground... Manchester United's Old Trafford.

They beat us 2-0 and we were out of the cup. The Rhyl players were celebrating wildly on the pitch and rightly so, but we were very down.

Over the three games, we had dominated them but we couldn't beat them. Maybe there was a little bit of complacency when it came to scoring the goals because the action didn't have the intensity of a normal league match.

It was embarrassing to lose to a non-league team.

It should have been an honour to play at Old Trafford but it's a bad memory for all of us. I still get people mentioning it to me today in Barnsley, 50 years on.

« CHAPTER 7 »

IN THE SUMMER of 1971, there were a lot of changes going on at Oakwell but I was oblivious to that and was just focusing on getting fit for the new campaign with an unusual method.

My neighbour, Keb Evans had two large greyhounds called Tina and Lassie.

That summer, I used to go running with them around the Cundy Cross area to keep fit before the season started.

I was so superstitious that I used to have to take them for a jog every Friday night; and I never made any other plans.

While I was doing that, Johnny Steele moved from manager to general manager, and John McSeveney came in as Barnsley manager.

It was a massive change for us. Steele had been in charge since 1960 and he was the only manager I had had at Oakwell. That was the same for pretty much all the other players.

I had played against McSeveney at Hull City's old ground, Boothferry Park. He was a left winger, so he came up against me a lot. He had been a very good player for Hull but we didn't know what he would be like in his first managerial job.

He had some new ideas. We used to go to a hotel before each game and he changed our pre-match meal from a poached egg on toast… to cornflakes and fruit.

On the pitch, he didn't seem to have the same impact on the team as Johnny

Steele had and we suffered as a consequence.

McSeveney was a good coach but he wasn't a manager.

It just didn't work out for him.

You get used to people and the way they work, and we were all used to Johnny Steele.

George Hamstead had moved to Bury and Barrie Thomas had to retire due to injury. Pat Howard, who had been a fantastic defender for us for years, was sold to Newcastle United early in the season and that left a massive hole in our team.

Throughout the history of the club, Barnsley have sold some great players and, most of the time, they have struggled to replace them.

We started with a 4-2 home win over Walsall but then we didn't win any of our next 13 matches, including four-goal home defeats to Aston Villa and Chesterfield.

We looked like we might have turned the corner with back-to-back wins down at Torquay United – coming from behind to win 2-1 after I scored an own goal – then at home to Oldham Athletic, but then we suffered through another 11-game winless run.

We would have some good spells but they were too short and we lacked consistency throughout the season.

We won three out of five games in a spell in February and early March to get out of the relegation zone for the first time since August, but we didn't win any of the next five.

Although we beat both Bolton Wanderers and Rochdale over the Easter weekend, we then didn't score in any of our next four matches, which brought only two points.

By the end of the season, the crowds had dropped to less than 2,000.

Eventually a 1-0 loss at Port Vale on the last day of the season sent us down on goal average.

The relegation was horrible and hard to take. We had worked so hard to get to the Third Division and establish ourselves at that level, and then we were back down to the basement division.

The mood around the team wasn't as good as it had been in the previous seasons. We weren't falling out with each other but we just couldn't seem to lift each other.

Jimmy Seal was our top scorer that season. He was a big strong lad and he had a bit of pace as well.

We had brought him in from Wolves the previous summer and he scored 12 goals but, when we went down, he moved on to York City.

I WAS NAMED Player of the Season in 1971/72.

It was a fantastic personal achievement. It was voted by the fans and, apparently, I won it by a record number of votes at the time. After the start I had at the club and the battle to be established in the team, it meant even more to be judged the club's No.1 player.

It didn't really take away any of the pain of relegation but it was nice to get that personal honour. Unfortunately, considering the season we had had, a bit of the shine was taken off that award.

IT WAS HARD being back in the Fourth Division.

You play the game to play at the best standard you can possibly reach, so to be back in the basement level of the Football League was disappointing.

The facilities were not very good at a lot of the clubs we visited, either.

I remember at Hartlepool, we came off the pitch covered in mud and there was one small bathtub waiting for us – and that was all the water we had to clean the whole team.

Also, at that level, players would get away with a lot of foul play. You could get away with some really bad tackles and lads got lumps kicked out of them. A lot of good players came through that league, though.

By that time, a lot of the players from the Barnsley teams of the late 1960s and early 70s had moved on and we struggled to recreate that team.

We were always trying to get back up from the Fourth Division. The attendances went down but a lot of the supporters stuck with us. We would have loved to have been higher up but it was still professional football and a good, competitive level.

Me? I was just really happy to still be a professional footballer.

Personally, I just went from strength to strength. I stayed in the team and I felt

I was improving all the time. I was well-known in the town and the community and a big part of the club.

A lot of people said to me that I was slowing down and my legs were going but I still stayed in the team and kept racking up the appearances. The press reminded me of every milestone I was approaching, as I got to 300... 400... 500 games and so on.

I was just trying to keep my standards up and to keep playing as long as I could. I was fortunate that I kept free from injuries.

I still felt good all the way into my late-thirties.

THE NEXT TIME I missed a match, after being dropped against Doncaster in 1970, was because of a suspension at the start of the 1972/73 season.

In pre-season, we used to play against teams from all over the world, like Hearts of Oak from Ghana... and also a Maltese side.

It was good experience as a team in the Third or Fourth Division to play against teams from all over the planet. The directors probably wanted us to have a different experience but those games didn't attract that many supporters.

This time, in the summer of 1972, we went on a tour of Scotland and I got sent off in a friendly match against Queen of the South.

The referee was lining us up to defend a free-kick and it was taking a while, and I let loose with my lip.

'Does he understand f*****g English?'

He sent me off.

My family couldn't believe it because they had never heard me swear, but you're a different person when you're on the pitch.

It wasn't a great time for the club; there had been a lot of frustration about the relegation a few months earlier and that probably just bubbled up in me.

Also, it was a friendly game and I maybe wasn't as disciplined or careful as I would have been in the league. The referees had been told to clamp down on behaviour like that for that season and obviously that worked against me.

The club appealed, which was very unusual.

I went up to Newcastle for an FA hearing but I was unsuccessful, and banned for three games.

It was really disappointing, especially because it was a friendly, but I probably should have just kept my mouth shut.

It was a stupid way to miss my first matches for a few years.

I still played the first few games of the 1972/73 season – including my 300th league start for the club in a 2-0 loss at Stockport County – because the appeal for my suspension was on hold due to postal delay.

Eventually, I was taken out of the team by the manager for a Sheffield Cup tie against Doncaster, ironically the same opponents for the last game I had missed nearly two years earlier.

McSeveney wanted to get the new back four used to playing together before the league games that I was suspended for. Centre-half Ray Pettit came in for me, and Paddy Greenwood moved to right-back. It was frustrating to be out of the team for a few weeks, for the first time in five years.

But I was soon back in.

I set up a goal on my return to the side, for a young player called Doug O'Connor, in a 3-2 home win over Peterborough United but we then didn't win any of our next four matches.

I conceded a controversial penalty in a 2-0 home loss to Darlington in October, 1972. It was a foul on a player called Colin Sinclair, who played against us for Darlington and then later Newport County, and I used to have some real battles with him.

It was a bit of a nasty rivalry.

We remembered each other from previous encounters.

That bad run led to John McSeveney being sacked in late October of 1972.

He had been in charge for less than 18 months, which was a very short spell for a manager in that era – especially at Barnsley. We were in danger of finishing in the relegation zone for the second season in-a-row and suffering the humiliation of having to apply for re-election to the Football League.

Johnny Steele was brought back in as manager for the rest of the season and he steadied the ship well. Nearly all the players knew Johnny and had faith in him.

I picked up a leg injury in a 0-0 draw at Torquay in January and, although I still managed to clear one off the line late on, I missed the next game which was a horrible 5-1 loss at Gillingham. Eric Winstanley was suspended for that match down in Kent and the team struggled without their two most experienced players.

Jim Iley came in as manager in April and he made a great start with a 4-1 win at Hartlepool with young striker Mick Butler hitting a hat-trick.

We also had a good 4-1 win at home to Lincoln City and finished the season 14th.

JIM ILEY WAS from nearby South Kirkby and had a good playing career with Tottenham Hotspur and Newcastle United.

He was the manager I played under who made us work the most. He had a coach called Mick Buxton and the two of them were very hard taskmasters who ran our legs off.

On a Monday morning, two days after playing a game, we used to run across the car-park, down Pontefract Road to Cundy Cross… around the roundabout… down Burton Bank… and up Harborough Hill – which is a very steep hill – and back into the ground.

It was a long, tough run.

There was a little shortcut which meant you could cut out a long portion of the route and a lot of us used to take it. What we didn't know, at first, was that Mick Buxton would be waiting in his car taking notes of who took the shortcut. When we got back to the ground, Jim Iley would know exactly who had cheated and he used to make those players do the run again.

It took us a long time to work out how he knew.

They used to take us up to Dorothy Hyman Stadium athletics track in Barnsley and make us run a lap in 75 seconds.

If you couldn't do it, you had to try again until you did it. It was torturous. There were other times when we were all eating our lunch in the canteen at the Dorothy Hyman Stadium and Iley would appear.

'The last one on the track does 20 press-ups!' he'd shout.

How some of the players didn't get killed in the rush I don't know. There was food and plates and chairs flying all over the place, people falling over; then you would feel queasy when you got out onto the track because you had been halfway through your meal.

We did it because we were frightened to death of him.

There used to be coal heaps on the Queens Ground, which is now the

Metrodome Leisure Centre, and he would make us run up and down them in pre-season. There were very, very steep and it was exhausting.

Jim and Mick would always be thinking of new ways to test our fitness and you never knew what was coming the next day. I was in my thirties by this point so I wasn't at my physical peak. But I was still the fittest and I still used to lead the way.

I got on with Jim very well and I think that was partly because I was always the best trainer and he used to use me as an example of how to train. Jim just wanted to do well in the game. He had come from a playing career in the top flight, and he was seriously ambitious.

He was a very hard trainer but it didn't do us any harm.

Jim was tough but fair.

He wasn't that popular with the fans because, ultimately, he wasn't successful. A lot of people didn't like him but – as far as I could see – the players and staff all got on well with him.

THE 1970s WASN'T the most successful era for Barnsley, until the last few years, but we still had some good players.

Ally Millar was an excellent midfielder. Johnny Steele went up to Scotland to sign him from Hamilton Academical when he was a teenager. He played his first game for Barnsley in the County Cup against Rotherham United and he took them apart.

He dominated the game from central midfield and myself and Eric and the other defenders behind him were watching and thinking... *Wow...what a player!*

He was the best on the pitch by far.

He carried on putting in good performances and played all the way through from 1971 to 1980 under John McSeveney, Jim Iley and Allan Clarke.

He had the talent to play in the First Division but he didn't like training very much. If he had worked a little bit harder, I think he would have got to the top level because he was a fantastic footballer. On his day, no one could get the ball off him and, if you passed to him, you would have a rest for five minutes.

One thing about Ally Millar that I never understood was that he used to use paperback books instead of shin pads. They would be thin books, and he opened them and placed them around his shin under his socks.

It seemed a very odd thing to do but it worked for him.

Left-back, Phil Chambers was another good player, with a very educated left-foot. He came from Ward Green in Barnsley and made his way through the Barnsley Boys, then the intermediates.

He played for the club for nearly as long as I did, from 1970 to 1985, making almost 500 appearances.

He was a good cricketer and, like Tony Leighton years before, he used to play at Shaw Lane on Friday nights and we'd all go to watch him. He used to hit balls into the allotments. He probably could have made it as a professional cricketer.

Les Lea was a wide right player.

He had been at Blackpool but he never got a game because he was the understudy to Stanley Matthews. He spent a few years at Cardiff, then moved to Barnsley in 1970. He stayed with us through the McSeveny era and most of Iley's reign.

He used to get teased because he drove a tiny little Ford Prefect. He was a good little winger and played more than 200 games. He had a lot of ability with good pace and used to put some good balls in from the right wing.

Mick Butler came from the Dodworth pit; he was an electrician down there as well as playing non-league football. All the locals always used to say, 'If you want a good striker… go to Dodworth pit'.

Mick came in for a trial and he was a natural – as sharp as a tack and a smashing striker. It was a similar story to me because I would have gone down the mines myself if I hadn't become a footballer. Both of us were determined not to go back down the pit if we had the chance to play football.

He did very well for the club. He scored goals for fun and was a revelation. The fans loved him because he was a local lad. I thought he would go all the way to the top but it never quite happened for him after he moved to Huddersfield Town.

John Manning was a massive lad. He was probably the strongest footballer I ever saw. He was built like Adebayo Akinfenwa, who plays for Wycombe Wanderers now. He would give defenders a nightmare because he was so big and strong.

John Peachey was another top target man.

He did well for the club and scored a lot of goals. He had a good partnership with Peter Price, another good striker. Price signed on Boxing Day, 1974 and, a week later, he scored a hat-trick in a 3-0 win over Southport.

Mick Pickering was a very good centre-half. He did very well for us; he was mobile and very hard.

Anton Otulakowski was a smashing little player. He came in from non-league football – as well as working for the Gas Board – in 1975 and did really well for us in midfield.

Later on, we had Brian Joicey, a big centre-forward who had been released by Sheffield Wednesday, whom he played for in the First Division. He was a big strong lad who could hold the ball up and head it well.

In those days you used to hit each other and Brian was getting so much flak in one game at York that they had to get the trainer on a couple of times. He went to the toilet at half-time and he started to pass blood.

He was rushed to hospital and, unfortunately, that was the end of his career. Defenders just used to get away with anything and they were very physical to a player like Brian who was so good. It was very sad that his career ended like that.

Towards the end of my playing career, we had a lad called Graham Pugh who had joined from Sheffield Wednesday.

You didn't want too many people like him around a club because he never took anything seriously and he was quite disruptive in training. When we were standing on the training ground, talking to the coaches about tactics, he would just pull someone's shorts down for no reason.

Looking back, it was funny, but at the time it could be quite frustrating and disruptive. But we did need people like him in our team because he could definitely play.

THERE WERE A few players who went from Barnsley to my boyhood club Newcastle in my time at the club.

Stewart Barrowclough was a very good young player for us who went on to be a great winger for them in the 1970s.

There was also Pat Howard, who was a fantastic centre-half and one of the best I ever played with. He played at the top level for Newcastle, and then Arsenal.

The other one was Martin Gorry, a very talented young full-back. When the Magpies had agreed a deal with Barnsley, I was told by the board to get on the train with him up to Newcastle and talk to him about controlling himself because he had a fiery temper and liked to spend time in discos.

I was a senior player at the time and Jim Iley wanted me to impress upon Martin that he had a fantastic opportunity.

We just wanted him to have the best possible chance and I was acting as his guardian. He signed but he didn't last that long up there.

For me, it was quite hard seeing other players being signed for Newcastle.

I really wished that it was me.

I would have loved to have played for my boyhood club and to have all my family and friends from Crookhall coming to watch me at St James' Park.

It would have been the ultimate dream.

I suppose I just wasn't quite good enough for the First Division. I think I could have thrived in the Second Division if we had been promoted again in the 1960s or early 70s but I was just a bit short of the quality you needed for the top flight.

JIM ILEY MADE a big call in the summer of 1973 to sell Eric Winstanley to Chesterfield for £15,000.

With all due respect to Chesterfield, it wasn't a destination or a fee worthy of such a fantastic footballer, man and servant to his hometown club for which he'd played for more than a decade. But Jim clearly wanted to go in a different direction and didn't see Eric's future at Oakwell.

We saw what we were missing straight away as, after moving on the Friday, he played against us for Chesterfield in a friendly on the Saturday and scored a typical header in a 1-1 draw.

We didn't start the 1973/74 season well, losing 1-0 at home to Colchester United in the opener, then 3-0 at Scunthorpe United in our first away game.

At Scunthorpe, I received the first and last red card of my career in a competitive match.

It was for fouling Neil Warnock.

He's known now as a manager but he was a winger back in the 1970s.

Neil would eventually be a teammate of mine at Barnsley, and a friend, but he was playing for Scunthorpe at the time. There was a 50/50 tackle and I whacked him.

He rolled and rolled and rolled... and screamed like a pig.

I was sent off.

It wasn't that bad a tackle; I probably made much worse challenges in my career. You would have thought I had taken most of his leg off.

That was Neil Warnock as a player; he used to fall over every time you touched him.

We were in the furthest corner of the pitch and I had to walk all the way across The Old Show Ground after my red card.

He was laughing at me as I was walking off, which I didn't like. He admitted later that I was unlucky to be sent off.

It was only half an hour into the game and the score was 0-0. But we ended up losing 3-0 and I remember sitting in the dressing-room, just devastated. It wasn't a nice experience to have to wait until the game was over, then see all my teammates trudge back in.

Later Neil moved to Barnsley and he was a good player for us, but he was a maungy swine.

He said in his autobiography that he felt he always had to play well when Barry Murphy was behind him at right-back. That's true!

I was shouting and rollicking him all the time.

Nobody liked playing against him but you liked having him on your team. He used to get a lot of free-kicks for us because he made a melodrama about every tackle.

We get on very well when I see him now.

He's one of the big characters that makes the game what it is. The sport needs people like Neil Warnock.

I WAS GIVEN a three-match suspension after that red card for the foul on Warnock, then struggled to get my place back in the team. A young lad called David Yates had come into the side and had done well during the suspension.

It was a strange feeling for me to be on the sidelines because I had been in the first team for nearly every game across seven years. But I was heading into my mid-thirties by this point and, although I knew I still had a lot to give, I accepted that I might not start every game.

Eventually, I got back in the side at centre-back over the Christmas period when Ray Pettit was injured.

We began 1974 with a 5-0 hammering of Scunthorpe on New Year's Day and it was nice to get a bit of revenge over them and, on a personal note, over Warnock. But I was in and out of the side for the rest of the season.

The team had only won one of the first 12 games of the season but gradually turned the form around and eventually finished 13th. At home, we were very good with a six-game winning run followed by one draw, then another seven straight wins. But our away form really let us down.

We only won twice on the road all season in the league, losing 16.

« CHAPTER 8 »

I HAD BEEN at the club for 12 years before I was officially made club captain.

It was at the start of the 1974/75 season.

An absolute honour.

After being out of the team for most of the previous season, Jim Iley's plan for me was to play mainly in the reserves and help to bring on some of the promising players who were coming through the youth system. He gave me the club captaincy as part of that.

But I had other ideas and, after impressing Jim in midfield in pre-season, I kept my place and got a lot of praise for my performances.

I had a lot to offer in terms of experience, and leadership. And I still had a little bit of skill. Jim was bringing through a lot of young players at that point and he looked to me to add a bit of know-how to the first team.

It felt like my career had a bit of a second wind.

It was good to prove everyone wrong, those who thought I was finished as a first team regular. Some fans and reporters said I was playing as well as I ever had.

The first game of the season was also my 350th league start for the club. We won it, 1-0 at home to Exeter City; then we won 3-0 at Swansea City, but we struggled to keep up that form.

We did have some decent results.

There was a 3-0 win at Reading after going two ahead in the first five minutes, but that was soon followed by a run of five successive defeats during which our star striker, Mick Butler suffered a broken leg.

We eventually got back on track with an excellent run of results over Christmas, thrashing Northampton 5-1, then winning 3-0 over both Stockport and Southport.

The second half of the season was mixed. We finished 15th.

MY TESTIMONIAL TOOK place on April 8, 1975.

It snowed all day.

Usually a player gets a testimonial match after 10 years at a club, but mine was after 13 seasons. Maybe that was because I didn't play much at all in the first five years.

Whatever the reason, I was just delighted to be recognised.

All the gate receipts went to me; that was the way testimonials worked back then.

The game was against Sheffield United, which was a big pull because they were in the top flight in that era.

We thought the weather would be decent in April but we had to cut the game down by 20 minutes due to the snow; it was continuous all day. It was described in the press as *"the worst blizzard of the year"* but, in Barnsley at least, it was just a wet slush which settled on the ground.

It was very disappointing.

Three busloads had come down from Consett.

It would have been called off if it had been a normal game.

But the attendance of 3,017 is still a lot of people to turn up in the snow.

Players like Mick Butler, Stewart Barrowclough, Pat Howard, Eric Winstanley, Peter Price and Brian Greenhoff all played in the game, and there was a guard of honour for me. It was a very proud moment for myself and my family.

We had a lot of ex-players playing before our game, well-known players from the 1940s and 50s and 60s, like Duncan Sharp, Harry Hough and Bobby Wood.

The day after, the sun came out and we managed to play a reserves game. It was a shame about the weather but it's still a day I look back on with a lot of pride.

Barnsley sent out letters to all the clubs in the country and I got letters back from most of them to wish me well, as well as contributions to the fund. My old friend from the North East, Laurie McMenemy, who was the Southampton manager then, sent £4.50 which was a lot of money in those days.

As well as that game, a lot of working men's clubs in Barnsley held special nights which I was invited to. They all wanted to put a show on for 'Barry Murphy's Testimonial'. I went to Ryhill, Wombwell, Darfield, Cudworth and a lot of other places in the borough. I was chuffed to bits because everybody, even the singers and comperes who did it for free, just wanted to get involved.

Every club was packed and it was great to see so many people turn out for me. I think the people of the town just appreciated all the effort I'd put in for the club over the years. I said a few words to thank them at each event.

There was a reception at the Civic Hall. There weren't enough hours in the day for people to put things on for me.

Ernest Dennis, the chairman, let me take the first team up to Consett. We opened a new club in Consett and played a game against an all-star team with players like Frank Clark, who was a long-serving Newcastle United player. It was brilliant for the people of Consett and there were more at that game than at the testimonial in Barnsley, simply because of the weather.

We played a cricket match against South Kirkby.

We got some celebrities to play in that as well.

Dickie Bird – the famous umpire from Barnsley who came with me to nearly all the events in my testimonial year – got us an autographed bat from the England and Australian teams at Headingley. They were seen signing it on TV and the commentator said, 'I wonder who he is getting that for?'

We raffled it off and my daughter won it, which was a bit awkward. But in all honesty, it wasn't a fix.

We played a series of different testimonial games and that, combined with me playing 37 times for the first team and nearly every week for the reserves, meant it might have been my busiest ever season.

SOMEONE WHO CAME with me to most of the events during my testimonial year – and did some comedy sets – was Charlie Williams, the Barnsley-born comedian and former footballer.

He was just appointed onto the board at Oakwell as I was made club captain.

There was a big story made of the fact that he had been appointed as a director. He had been a footballer for Doncaster Rovers before he became a comedian. 'I was never the best player in the world,' he used to say, 'but I could stop those who were.'

He had made a lot of headlines and history by being one of the first black footballers, and then a celebrity entertainer, and he was a very big name back in those days. Being on the board was good publicity for Charlie as well as Barnsley Football Club. He was fantastic for the club.

I got on very well with him – he was very funny, but also a nice man. He used to go with us to away games on the bus, and people recognised him much more than they recognised us. He always spoke to people and he used to call everyone, 'Me old flower'.

Charlie was one of the really great characters I met in my career and I remember him very fondly.

FOR THE 1975/76 season, once again I was due to drop back into the reserves and help the young players develop.

But I knew I could contribute to the first team and, after filling in at right-back because David Yates was injured, I played at centre-back and then central midfield.

I was happy with my own performances but, as a team, we were struggling.

Bob Doyle, a midfielder, started the season as captain of the team, and I was club captain. Bob was a good player but he wasn't captain material. They sacked him and made me captain of the team as well as club captain.

I had the armband for most of the rest of my career. I just had an attitude which managers obviously liked. I wanted to win everything and I could gee the other players up.

It came quite easily to me to be that big, loud voice on the training pitch, and in games. I would soon get even more responsibility.

IN NOVEMBER 1975, we lost at Merseyside to non-league Marine in the FA Cup.

I was on the bench, watching on in horror.

They kicked lumps out of our team. We didn't adapt to it and they deserved to win. It wasn't a good experience to sit and watch that game.

Jim Iley was under quite a lot of pressure. We had won only once in the league since August and were facing the prospect of a relegation battle.

Mick Buxton, the coach, had left earlier in the season and the chairman Ernest Dennis thought Jim needed some help. Gerry Young, a very experienced coach, was brought in from Sheffield Wednesday and I was also brought onto the coaching staff for the first time.

The club needed to bring in an experienced coach and that was Gerry. I was there to help Gerry and Jim, and also to learn a lot from them. It was a big honour for me that the board thought I could add something as a coach as well as a player.

You didn't have to get loads of badges to be a coach in those days, you just needed one preliminary badge. Then you could get a job. I went on a one-day course at Barnsley Technical College.

There were classroom sessions and coaching sessions in a big gymnasium. Ray Wood, the ex-Manchester United, England and Barnsley player, took the class.

The results started to pick up from that point. We had a strong second half of that season and finished well clear of the relegation zone, in 12th.

On a personal note, I passed Eric Winstanley's club record of 461 appearances on March 30, 1976 in a 4-0 home win over Cambridge United.

Earlier that month, in a 3-1 win at home to Newport County, one of the visiting players went over the top of the ball and tackled me very badly. It left me with a big gash down my leg. I still wasn't right for the next few games but I played anyway and broke the record.

To break Eric's record was a big moment for me because he was a close friend of mine. When I did it, he brought me a bottle of wine, which was a fantastic gesture.

A COUPLE OF weeks later, we won 7-1 at Workington on a Wednesday in April. John Peachey scored a hat-trick and Peter Price got two.

It was one of those games when everything went in.

There weren't many teams that got results like that in those days. We travelled there and back on the same day, like we did to every club expect the ones down in

Devon.

The result was being announced in working men's clubs throughout the evening. People who had been in different clubs all told me that was how they heard about it.

◄ ◄ ◆ ▷ ►

Eric Winstanley was one of the first friends Barry made when he arrived at Barnsley and joined him in the formidable defence of the late 1960s. Barry eventually surpassed Eric's appearance record for the club.

THE DAY BARRY broke my record, I went to Oakwell and took him a bottle of wine. I was really pleased for him and he completely deserved it.

I knew it had been quite a difficult journey for him to get to that point. In his early days, he was frustrated about not playing more. He seemed very close to leaving and that would have been the worst thing that could have happened to him and to the club.

I always had a good friendship with Barry, like all of us did at the club in those days.

There was a lot of comradeship at that time. We were all on pretty similar wages so there were no problems or divides in that respect.

We used to go out together; we were all mates, we all went to each other's weddings and we started families at a similar time.

We would be out for a drink and Barry would suddenly get up to sing a Geordie song. We called him 'The Geordie Yodeller'.

I have seen him get up in loads of different clubs and pubs when there was music on and start singing. I have had plenty of drinks out of him because people would buy us all a round.

I don't know whether he is a good singer but he had the confidence to get up and do it.

He was always enthusiastic and bright and cracking jokes but, when it came to his football, he was very serious because he loved the game.

It took him a long time to settle down at Oakwell and get the best out of himself. He had come from non-league football. He was strong but it was only later with experience that he became a lot better on the ball.

What was always there was his fitness.

That gave him the ability to last a long time and play a lot of games.

He was always at the front of the group if we were running, with his chest out. And he was one of those lucky players that never seemed to get injured. He was still one of the best, even when he was well into his thirties and I used to go back to Barnsley to watch them.

He just got better and better with experience.

As he went on, he got more and more popular with the fans too.

When other managers came to the club, they respected players who had been there a lot of years because they wanted them to be the experience behind the team. He was a big help for all the managers who came along after I left.

I am told Barry scored three goals in his career and, to be honest, I am surprised he scored that many. I remember once in a training game, there was a penalty and he insisted on taking it. He put it well wide, then just ran back into his position at the back without looking at any of us, as we were all laughing quietly.

I joined Barnsley in 1960 after I left school and, within two years, I was playing first team football because the captain Duncan Sharp retired.

Barry came to the club at a similar time and he was this Geordie lad who was just a bit older than us as apprentices. He came down as a centre-half but was moved to right-back and played in the reserves for quite a few seasons.

He was a little bit older and had the experience of playing for South Shields.

He did a great job developing players he played with in the reserves; that was the important role he had at the club.

He was irritated that he wasn't playing first team football and he used to tell me how frustrated he was. I remember one time he told me he was going to see the manager, Johnny Steele and ask for a move. But I told him he was respected at Barnsley and that he should fight for his place.

Eventually, he got in the first team and we were teammates for a good many years. He became one of the best full-backs at that level.

The promotion season of 1967/68 was special.

When I was at school and watching Barnsley in the early 1950s, they were always in the Second Division and they had fantastic players, like Tommy Taylor. So, for us to be down in the Fourth Division was difficult for me and a lot of other Barnsley fans to stomach.

We had also just nearly gone under as a club. It was a bad time.

You had reporters knocking on your door to try to find out something out about the club. It was very difficult for everyone, so it was great to get promoted the next year.

We played with a back four which was quite unusual at that time because most teams played with a back three and wing-backs. Norman Rimmington and Johnny Steele worked really hard in training on making us a good back four; we knew how to play with each other and cover each other.

That was the first time that coaching became really important in English football and also at Barnsley because formations were changing, and the game was getting a lot more technical and tactical. Norman had just got his coaching badges and did a great job at schooling us.

The onus was on us, as a defence, to be the backbone of the team.

Barry was the oldest of the four of us but, even though he wasn't a local lad like me, Pat Howard or Eric Brookes, he was very passionate about the club and worked extremely hard.

We didn't give many goals away, we were always talking and organising.

I had been out for two years because I injured my cruciate ligaments at Luton Town in 1965.

I was told later that Bill Nicholson, the Tottenham Hotspur manager, was at the game and a deal was in place to sign me. Johnny Steele said I was the unluckiest player in the world.

I have been told since that Manchester United and Liverpool were also interested.

That's football, injuries happen sometimes.

I am just glad I came back because, in those days, you were usually finished with that injury.

Once I came back, we got the promotion and I was playing well again but a lot of people said that no club would take a chance on me with 'that knee' and there were doubts if I would pass a medical.

QPR and Norwich City still came in for £40,000 and £50,000 but they were turned down.

Sheffield United, who had just sold Mick Jones to Leeds United, offered £65,000 and two players but again it was turned down.

I had a word with Johnny Steele and the chairman, and told them I wanted to go.

When you have been so close to the top level, and had it taken away, you want to take any chances you get. But then the offers dried up for a couple of seasons and eventually I got frustrated and asked for a transfer.

I moved to Chesterfield, partly because I didn't want the burden on my shoulders any more of being captain of my hometown club. It weighed quite heavily on me.

Barry was captain of Barnsley later on.

He loved it at Oakwell because he was accepted and respected. He became like a Barnsley person after being there for all those years.

When I go to watch Barnsley, I go to see him in the Legends Suite.

Barry saw through all the bad times and good times, and was a great servant for the club as a player, then a coach.

And now he continues in that role as an ambassador.

« CHAPTER 9 »

AT THE START of the 1976/77 season, we were drawn away at West Ham in the second round of the League Cup.

That was after playing York City three times in the first round and beating them 2-1 in the third game, having drawn the first two 0-0.

West Ham were one of the best teams in the country at the time. They had world class players like Billy Bonds and Trevor Brooking. All the big teams played their full-strength sides in those days, even in the cups against lower league sides, and they never rested their star players.

West Ham showed their quality and won 3-0.

I remember saving a shot off the line at 2-0, but Pat Holland tapped in his second goal of the game to make it three.

It was always disappointing to lose but we were pleased to have shared a pitch with the likes of Brooking and we certainly didn't disgrace ourselves.

We had another brush with fame later in 1976, as myself and most of my first team colleagues were on TV on *It's No Joke Living in Barnsley* with the actor Brian Glover, who had made his name in the film *Kes*.

He was from Barnsley and the programme was about him going around the town and meeting various people.

The production company got in touch with the football club and they were allowed to come down to Oakwell and do some filming. It was up to me, as captain, to get the players together. When the film crew came down we did a training session with Brian.

The footage is funny because he's struggling to keep up with us and very out of breath while talking to the camera.

We all went into the baths afterwards and they filmed us talking about our training session. I was sitting next to him and we had to splash him as he was trying to talk to the camera.

It was a good afternoon.

IN THE LEAGUE, we spent most of the 1976/77 season in or near the promotion positions.

After a few disappointing seasons, Iley was starting to get decent results. We were excellent at home, winning 16 of our 23 games including six in-a-row from December to late February. But our away form again let us down, especially in the first half of the season.

We lost our first five matches away from home and only scored four in the first 10.

We suffered a double blow early in the season when two of our best players were bought by other clubs. We went to Southport on a Friday night in October and the bus back didn't leave until 3am because West Ham's manager John Lyall was there to sign Anton Otulakowski, who had made a fantastic start to the season.

Newcastle came in for Martin Gorry at pretty much the same time and, suddenly, we had lost two excellent young players. I had started the season back at right-back but then I replaced Anton in central midfield for a few games before moving back to right-back in place of Martin.

Even though I turned 37 during this season, I played every game and felt I contributed a lot. John Saunders took over as captain midway through the season, but I remained club captain.

I played my 500th game in a 3-2 win at Rochdale in January, 1977. It was also my 450th league game. There was a big fuss and a presentation, because I had reached the milestone.

The board of directors bought me a silver tea service.

The players bought me silver goblets on a silver tray.

It was always 'something' if you were invited into the board room.

I had a guard of honour of players onto the pitch for the next home game. The press cameras were there. I was captain of the team.

It was brilliant.

WE HAD SOME great moments that season like a 5-1 home win over Scunthorpe, with John Peachey scoring a hat-trick, as well as a five-game winning run in late January and early February.

Brian Joicey was one of the top scorers in the division that season and he had passed 20 goals by February and ended up with 29, while we had some good midfield players like Neil Warnock, Mick Pickering, Ally Millar and Kenny Brown.

We had been in the four promotion places for most of 1977 and, in our third from last game, we went 3-0 up at home to Exeter, who were one of our promotion rivals. But, somehow, they came back and won 4-3.

It was awful.

We had only lost one home game all season and none of our previous 13 at Oakwell.

Exeter didn't bring their change strip with them so we played in white and they played in our red kits. People used to say we looked like Real Madrid at first in the white kits, with the way we played, but we let it slip.

We were cheered off at half-time and booed off at full-time.

We just thought the game was over at 3-0, but credit to Exeter. That game killed us off in our promotion chase. We won our last two games but came sixth – four points outside the promotion positions – and Exeter went up.

On a personal note, I had played every game of that season for the first time since the 1971/72 campaign. I was playing better at that point than I had for nearly a decade.

I felt I had a new lease of life. I was motivated by being written off by some fans and some people at the club, who had expected me to be phased out of first team action after being made player/coach two seasons before.

But I was still playing well enough to keep my place.

No one in the press or any of the fans knew how old I was. There was no internet... no Google, like there is now. And I just used to say that I was older than 30.

I liked to keep them guessing.

But I knew the end of my playing career was coming so I just wanted to make the most of every game.

‹ ‹ ◆ ▷ ▶

Neil Warnock holds the record for most promotions as a manager in English football, with eight. He says the highlight of his playing career was a two-year spell at Oakwell from 1976-78 when Barry Murphy was captain.

IT'S AMAZING THAT Barry Murphy made 569 appearances for Barnsley, while only passing to his teammates 10 times.

I say that with tongue in cheek because no one plays that many games without being a good player and having a great attitude.

What he lacked in ability, he made up for in effort and heart. He never gave up and he hated to see any other player not giving one hundred percent effort. There were one or two heated discussions in the dressing-room because of that. He would let it be known who wasn't pulling their weight, which is what you want from a captain.

I played the best football I ever played when I was playing with Barry. He was the right-back and I was the right winger.

He was such a good captain and he was brilliant for me. He encouraged me and supported me all the time. He had so much energy and drive.

Barry always wanted Barnsley to be the best and that really lifted everyone. He was such a bubbly character; I loved his sense of humour. His personality would rub off on everyone else at the club.

In my second season, 1977/78, I had my best ever campaign with 10 goals from the wing.

Only Brian Joicey got more goals than me for Barnsley that season. It was all down to Barry.

He got me working hard; he taught me how to help him out on the right-hand side. It was just fabulous for me. Playing with him was the most fun I had as a player.

Everything seemed to come from the right side because we had such a good partnership.

I didn't enjoy playing against him so much.

You didn't want to play against him as a winger because he was like a rash. He would never leave you alone.

I remember the time I played against him for Scunthorpe and he got sent off for a tackle on me. It was the only time he got sent off in his career in a competitive game.

Barry claims that I made a meal out of the tackle and conned the referee into giving him a red card.

He is one hundred percent correct.

I writhed around in pretend agony until he got his marching orders... then I got up.

That tackle was the only way he could stop me because I was too quick and too good for him on that day.

We have a laugh and joke about it now but I don't think he was very happy with me at the time.

Once I moved to Barnsley, we got on very well.

He took the Mickey out of everyone.

I had a fruit and veg shop in Sheffield alongside my football career. If I ever made a mistake or had a bad game, Barry would say, 'It's a good job you've got a fruit and veg shop because you won't be playing football long'. But he was only joking.

He would always have something to say about your clothes or your appearance.

If you walked in with a top of a certain colour on, he would ask you why you were wearing your grandmother's clothes... and what was she was wearing?

But, when the training started, he was very serious and there was no messing about then. He was nearly 40 but he was still super fit and leading the way in training.

If you had a problem, you would go to Barry and he would sort it out. He was like a father figure to me.

He was the heart of the dressing-room.

He would talk the same to the cleaning lady as he would to the chairman. He didn't suffer fools gladly and he said things as he saw them.

It was good to have someone like Barry to keep us all together because the manager, Jim Iley was a bit strange. Jim had been a good player and, even though he was in his forties, he still had the best ability at the club. He was the best in all our training drills even though he was the manager.

He ruled a bit by fear with the youngsters, which I didn't like. I had a few rollickings off him… like most of the players did. But you just had to learn from it.

I didn't play that much in my first season. I remember being told by the girl in the office that I was going to get released, before anyone had told me officially.

So, I went in to see Jim Iley and told him I would like to go part-time for the next season, train a couple of days and take a drop in wages. He had obviously made up his mind to get rid of me but he thought about it and gave me a part-time contract.

I managed to talk myself into another year because of the girl in the office.

I worked for Combined Insurance Company of America, who used to insure most of the players. I used to go around Barnsley, especially Wombwell, selling insurance door-to-door. I got recognised sometimes. You can't imagine that happening with a player now. I played my best football when I had that job.

But then I moved on to York City and eventually became a manager.

Whenever I come back to Barnsley as a manager, Barry is there waiting for me. We always have a good laugh. He never seems to change.

He still looks well and he has the same personality.

In Barnsley, everyone knows him and he has an aura about him.

I was fortunate enough that I met Norman Rimmington and Barry Murphy, who were both absolutely dedicated to Barnsley FC and were people that no one had a bad word to say about.

No one will play as many games as Barry did for Barnsley… ever.

◄ ◁ ◆ ▷ ►

THE 1977/78 SEASON was my last as a player.

We started off with a 4-1 loss at lower league, Chesterfield in the League Cup and, although we won the second leg 3-0, we lost the replay at Oakwell and missed out on a second-round game against top flight Manchester City.

Those games brought the first senior matches in the career of Mick McCarthy, who would go on to be one of Barnsley's greatest ever players. He was only a teenager at the time but he fitted into our team straight away at centre-back and had a lot of confidence.

He was a pleasure to play with and the fans took to him immediately because he was a local lad.

You knew he would make it to the top as soon as you trained with him.

He wanted to win everything.

You would always pick him first in training if you were being split into teams. He always wanted to win and he had a tremendous appetite for the game. He had a fantastic attitude, he would always tell you off if you weren't doing what he wanted... even if he was half your age.

He was a winner and he would never settle for second best. Every day, he wanted to stay late after training and do extra work.

We used to have to throw balls up for him so he could practice his heading. It meant a lot to him to play for his hometown club Barnsley.

He was a proper centre-half and not many players got past him.

But he was also a good technical footballer.

I roomed with Mick and we got on very well.

It was my last season and his first season. I think they put us together so I could talk a bit of sense to him and keep an eye on him in a nice way.

Personally, I would still put Eric Winstanley and Pat Howard ahead of him as Barnsley's best centre-backs ever. They were slightly better footballers but Mick was an absolute winner and that got him to the level he eventually reached – in the First Division and internationally with the Republic of Ireland.

That season, I played with both Mick and Neil Warnock in the same team. I would never have thought then that they would both go on to be top managers for many decades to come, but they were both good lads whom I got on with very well at the time.

THE LEAGUE SEASON began with a 4-0 win at home to Rochdale, in which I scored my third and final goal from the penalty spot.

I missed one a couple of weeks later, at home to Newport County after Neil Warnock was fouled, but we still won 1-0. I was taken off penalty duties a few weeks later once Brian Joicey got the winning spot-kick in a 3-2 success at home to Hartlepool.

Once again, our away form let us down as, even though we were very good at Oakwell and won our first six league games there, we were only victorious three times on the road all season.

We were unbeaten in 14 league matches, from October until February, and began 1978 in second place after a 2-1 New Year's Day win over Darlington in which I managed to clear two off the line.

But a five-match winless run saw us drop out of the top four and, after another decent run, three defeats in-a-row in April pretty much finished our chances.

I missed a 2-0 loss at Brentford which was the first time I was out of the side for 116 games in more than two years, then I was in and out through injury for the last month.

After a 2-0 home loss to Swansea City, we knew we weren't going to finish in the top four. That was also my last ever game at Oakwell as well as being Jim Iley's last as manager, as he resigned to take over at Second Division Blackburn Rovers with three games left in the season.

My last match for Barnsley, although I didn't know it at the time, was a 3-1 loss at Torquay United. I could have been sent off for handballing on the line but no penalty was given as one of their players tapped in the rebound.

I managed to clear one off the line later... the final time I would ever do that.

And that was it.

After 569 games, my time as a Barnsley player was over.

AS WELL AS football, I used to play a few other sports at amateur level.

I played squash in the Yorkshire League, alongside my career at Oakwell. It was hard work but good for your fitness and reflexes.

I used to play twice a week at a club on Twibell Street in Barnsley town centre, then later I joined Shaw Lane Sports Club. These days, clubs probably wouldn't let professional footballers play squash because you could get an injury. But I never did.

I would never play if we had a game the day after.

All the squash players I came up against knew who I was. I didn't like to lose and I was very competitive. Ray McHale, another Barnsley player, would also play in that league later on.

I carried on playing when I was a coach at Leeds and I kept playing into my late seventies, but then it was racquetball which is for older people.

I also played for Cudworth Cricket Club in the Barnsley Sunday League. I was an all-rounder. Every bowler I came up against wanted to get me out and the batters all wanted to hit me for six, because of who I was.

I didn't play that many matches because I needed to be at home with my family on some weekends when the football season wasn't on.

When you are a sportsman, you tend to be able to pick up other sports – especially if they are ball sports because it is all about hand-eye co-ordination.

◄ ◄ ◆ ► ►

Neil Murphy, Barry's son, reflects on growing up as the child of an Oakwell hero.

AS A KID, I used to think Barnsley was a much bigger town than it is because it used to take us ages to get anywhere.

Everybody wanted to stop and talk to my dad, and he was happy to do so.

Everybody knew him, and that's still the case now.

To us, it was just normal. He was just my dad. He played football like other people's dads did other jobs.

That was just how it was.

It was nice to see that he was so loved.

Barnsley were a Fourth Division team so there wasn't a lot of glamour involved. But we seemed to open a lot of summer fetes and galas. I just thought that was what everyone did.

I spent some time as a kid, during the summer holidays, watching Barnsley train. I would fetch the ball from down the banking at the Queens Ground when it went down.

We went to every home game as a family.

I can't remember many games, just that it was quite a difficult time for the club and the fans would sometimes be calling for Jim Iley's head.

I was 10 when my dad retired so I remember the times when he was a coach more clearly.

When he was coach of the under-18s, which he loved, I went on a few away days with them on a Saturday morning; then we would get back for the first team game.

The club seemed to change under Allan Clarke and get a lot more up to date and professional and better organised. They had a great team and there was a buzz in the town.

At school, sometimes people were interested in talking about my dad because he was a player, then a coach.

Then he went to Leeds United and, all of a sudden, my dad had a job in the First Division.

You could call it a character-building experience, being at school in Barnsley when your dad moves to Leeds.

Before that, no one talked about my dad on a daily basis, but then everyone started talking about him all the time and giving me a lot of stick.

They called him 'reject' and 'traitor' which were both quite ironic.

People gave me quite a lot of grief but I just wore a Leeds scarf every day and thought… Come on… let's have it.

It's family first.

We didn't see much of him in those years because he was up and gone first thing in the morning, then at Leeds all day and often scouting or coaching at night or on a weekend.

When you are in a big job like that, and you care a lot, it is a lot of pressure and it takes up nearly all of your time. But it was a great experience for him.

Leeds did really well at first but they got relegated in 1982 so I got even more stick at school.

They were in the same division as Barnsley. The Reds won the derby the next season so I was dreading school the following Monday.

My dad is a very honest person. He didn't watch me play football much but I remember one time he came to see me play for the school. Looking back now, I can say I was a very average player but as a kid of about 13, which I was at the time, you dream of being a professional, especially if your dad is one.

He showed up in the Leeds United Ford Cortina.

He watched me play; then I got in the car with him to go home. I started talking to him about which position I should play.

'I don't think I am quick enough to play up front,' I told him. 'But I don't want to play in defence. Maybe I should stick to playing in midfield.

'What do you think I should do?"

Dad looked at me... 'I think you should be an electrician,' he then said.

'People will always need electricians.'

That sums him up, you ask him a straight question and get a straight answer. It certainly put me straight in terms of my future footballing aspirations.

The closest I got was going to games at Barnsley and Leeds when my dad was the coach.

I remember going to Elland Road and seeing all the photos of the glory years and the trophies.

I used to hang out outside the changing-rooms and get all the opposition players' autographs. I have a really good collection of signatures from the best players in the country in the early 1980s.

Denis Irwin was an apprentice and I would chat to him while he was mopping the corridor.

My uncle Brian used to come to all the games at Barnsley, and then Leeds, and I would sometimes watch with him. At Leeds, he would often be with someone who I just knew as John.

One time, the three of us went to a Leeds game at Oakwell and a Barnsley fan walked up, with his son, to John and told his son, 'This is the great John Charles... the best player I've ever seen'.

I had no idea he was the former Leeds and Juventus striker.

The club ambassador role that my dad does now – hosting on matchday – has been really good for him.

He loved playing at Barnsley, being part of the club and being seen as a one-club man. He loves being recognised as part of the community.

I am probably more proud of him for that than his playing career.

He had a brother who worked in the mines and a brother who worked in the steelworks so he appreciated every day that he got to work in football. There have been players who were a lot better but I think one of the reasons he is so well-loved is because he puts in, as he would say, one hundred and ten percent effort.

From my point of view, it's great to have someone like that in your corner throughout your life.

There is nothing I could do that would be wrong in his eyes.

I took my family to live in Australia in 2011, because an opportunity had come up through work. I knew it broke his heart but he was very supportive.

He came to visit us in Brisbane, the furthest he's been in his life, and he loved it and said it was a 'fantastic opportunity'.

Then, when I told him we were coming back a few years later, he said, 'I should think so... I never liked it in the first place'.

He just supports me no matter what.

PART THREE

The Clarke Revolution

« CHAPTER 10 »

TAP, TAP... TAP.

TAP, TAP... TAP.

TAP, TAP... TAP.

THE EXPENSIVE SHOES made a loud noise on the Oakwell corridor as our famous new manager walked down to the dressing-room to meet us.

As club captain, I'd been asked to get all the players together.

I had everyone in the dressing-room.

Waiting.

TAP, TAP... TAP.

TAP, TAP... TAP.

We'd all seen Allan Clarke on TV playing for England and Leeds United, and he had been one of the most famous players in the country in the 1970s. And we were all very much taken aback that he had decided to come to Barnsley... to come down to the Fourth Division, and we didn't exactly know what to expect.

He walked in the door and I thought it was Jesus Christ himself.

He was wearing a grey mohair suit and white shoes. He looked a million dollars. And then he spoke to all the players.

We were all speechless.

AT THE END of the 1977/78 season, with Jim Iley having left, we had all been waiting to see who would be appointed as manager.

There were never really any secrets at that point, and it was known for a while that Allan was in contention for the job. Everyone was excited about it, then eventually we found out he had got the job and we knew we were going places.

It gave the players a massive lift to know that they would be playing for him and with him as player/manager. The fans and everyone in the town were so excited that such a big name had come to Barnsley.

It had been a tough decade for the town and the club, with us mainly being in the Fourth Division and the attendances getting smaller.

But everything changed under Allan.

He revitalised the club.

He made it so much more professional. Ernest Dennis, the chairman, had done very, very well to get him to come to the club but Allan had always wanted to be a player/manager and he was given the chance to do that at Oakwell.

He served his apprenticeship as a manager at Barnsley and learned a lot.

He encouraged the players to go into the community a lot more. I had always done that but the whole squad were doing it under Allan and it made us much more of a community club.

Even Allan's attitude to players' wives was very different.

Before he arrived, they were lucky to get a seat or a cup of tea at half-time but then he changed all of that and made sure they were looked after.

When he took us away to Marbella in pre-season, he sent flowers and a box of chocolates to each of the wives.

Allan made sure that every single person at the club felt appreciated and, being such a big name, it gave them all a big lift, and made them more motivated and passionate in their jobs.

The way he used to talk to us was fantastic.

Even with the people who worked in the laundry or on the ground staff, he'd make sure he spoke to them and treated them well and fixed any little problem they might have. No one had done that before. That approach made a massive difference to every single person.

He was great in training too.

The things he used to do with the ball and the goals he used to score were like nothing we had seen before. He never asked the players to do anything he couldn't do.

He brought a lot of his ideas in from Don Revie, who he had played under at Leeds.

The players trained with a ball all the time under Allan, which was very different to Jim Iley, who made us do a lot of running.

We used different formations, and thought about tactics a lot more than under previous managers. Training was all about skills and developing techniques instead of just fitness.

Allan was also red-hot on discipline.

If someone didn't do what the boss wanted, that player would soon change his mind if he wanted to play.

If Allan didn't think the players had given one hundred percent in training in the morning, he would bring them back in the afternoon for an extra session.

His appointment and the way he changed the club started an upward trajectory that, a few decades later after some ups and downs, would lead to Barnsley getting to the Premiership.

ONCE HE HAD been introduced to the players on his first day, Allan Clarke pulled me in to the office and said that he didn't see me as a first team player – he wanted me to look after the intermediate teams.

I was the oldest player in the Football League at that time and I did feel as though the time had come for me to stop playing for the first team.

Allan was looking to build a team which didn't include me, and I understood that. But he wanted to keep me involved in the club. I had to accept it and, deep down, I knew he was right.

At 38, I had done enough.

When you have played that many games, you don't want to give in but, eventually, you know when your time is up.

If you were involved in football, you knew your career had to come to an end sometime. I said that I understood the decision but that I would like to continue playing for the reserves and bring the young lads through on the pitch. Allan agreed to that.

He also wanted me to be a youth team coach for the club. He put me in charge of the under-18s, who were also known as the intermediates.

It was simple to get the qualifications but it wasn't easy to make the transition from first team player to youth team coach.

I was still involved in the game, which was fantastic, but you do miss playing and you become a different man. I had to remind myself that being a coach was the next best thing to playing.

You have to be in charge of a team and you change as a person.

I enjoyed it because I could see the young players developing. That gave me a lot of satisfaction.

And we were winning games against the under-18s sides of good, top flight clubs. I felt I was contributing to the football club.

I was also helping Allan in first team training and games when he needed me, but my main focus was on the youth team.

In our first season together, my intermediates team won the Northern Intermediate League – which was a very good standard – and the Challenge Cup. It was the first time the club had ever won the Intermediate League.

Two of our last three league games were against Newcastle United, who had also reached the cup final which was due to be played over two legs, so we agreed the fixtures would count towards both competitions.

We drew 0-0 at home but we had not lost away all season and I was confident the lads would get the job done up in the North East. We won 2-0 thanks to goals by Graham Reed and Gary Smith.

We went all over Europe to tournaments, including a very prestigious one in Düsseldorf, at the end of the season which we won against some very good sides. Our oldest player was 19 and it was an under-23 tournament, so to win it was a fantastic achievement.

NONE OF THAT success was down to me, it was all because of the lads.

I got on very, very well with them and I was just myself with them. I treated them like adults and they liked that. I think they appreciated that I had played a lot of games for Barnsley and I knew what it took to make it.

It turned into a very enjoyable period of my career.

We had a trophy presentation at the end of the season, attended by Allan Clarke and all the directors. It meant a lot to the club to win that league for the first time.

To have that much success in my first season in the role, and at the same time as the first team were getting promotion, was fantastic and I was pleased that my first year after playing brought so much success.

We would use the same system and tactics as the first team and work very hard with them on positioning and organisation.

Allan Clarke told me not to feel sorry for the intermediate players.

One day, the first team had gone away to London and our team played really well and got a big win so I said they didn't have to mop up the dressing-rooms, as they usually would.

The next day, after Allan had come back, there was a note on the blackboard in the dressing-room.

'When the cat's away, the mice will play,' it said.

He moaned to me about it and told me not to let them get away with anything no matter how well they played.

I never let that happen again.

THE MAIN PART of my job was to bring kids through and get them ready for the first team, and we had some real gems whom Allan Clarke would slowly bring into his side.

Some of them didn't make it, of course.

Our top scorer that season was Alan Billingham. But he never made a first team appearance. He was an excellent striker, always in the right place at the right time, however he was too thin and frail to make it in first team football.

Others, however, went on to have great careers.

David Speedie was a fantastic little player, who went on to have a top-level career. He combined playing for the youth team with a job as a window cleaner and a spell down the mines at Brodsworth Colliery.

Unfortunately, it didn't really work out for him under Allan Clarke and he had to move on.

He played in midfield for us, then his next club Darlington played him up front and Chelsea signed him for big money. He later played for Liverpool and was a Scotland international.

Graham Reed had gone to the same school as Speedie in Adwick.

They were best mates, Reedy and Speedie. Reed made a big impact as a 17 year-old when he scored two goals in the FA Cup against Worksop Town. Unfortunately, he could not stay in the team and never made it at Barnsley.

The star of that team was Ian Banks.

He was a local lad and he became a fantastic player for Barnsley.

He was a very good midfielder with a great mentality. As soon as I saw him, I knew he would play for the first team. He was skilful, strong and he could smash a ball with either foot. He was also a stocky lad, but fast.

He read the game very, very well. He didn't seem fazed at all by moving up to the first team and settled in straight away to the pace of professional football.

I would always try to coach Banksy to tackle and run back, but he wouldn't have any of it.

He just wasn't defensive-minded at all. But he got away with it because he was a fantastic attacking player.

He was the best striker of the ball I have ever seen.

He was a natural. He did very, very well for himself by moving on to Leicester City.

The likes of Banksy were already in the youth system when I became coach but I also had the free time to go and sign players.

My first signing for the under-18s was Joe Joyce from my hometown, Consett. I saw him play when I went back up for a weekend.

He was playing a match in Consett and I liked what I saw so I got permission from Allan Clarke to sign him. He was about to go to university in Liverpool and his mother didn't want him to sign. But eventually I persuaded her to let him give football a chance and he was a massive success, playing 388 games over 12 years.

He made his debut in the 7-0 loss at Reading but he showed great resilience to bounce back from that. Joe was the best bit of business I was involved in and, in my opinion, one of the best in the club's history.

WE USED TO get letters all the time from players asking for trials and I used to invite them all to practice matches on a Sunday afternoon.

One of them was Paul Longden, a left-back, who played quite a few matches for Barnsley's first team.

I also signed Winston Campbell.

He had impressed me at one of our practice matches, so I went down to Ecclesall Road in Sheffield where he lived. It was a big terraced house with kids running all over the place. They were a lovely family who had raised a really nice lad in Winston. They didn't hesitate in signing the contract and he was soon a Barnsley player.

He was the first black player to play for the club in a league game, and I joke that that is another club record I helped to break. But it was all down to Winston and his talent.

He had a lot of ability and he was as hard as nails.

Defenders used to bounce off him.

I don't think it was easy for him, or any of the other black players, at that time. They had to endure a lot and it couldn't have been nice for the kid. I can't recall any specific incidents involving Winston but there was a lot of racism going on, which is terrible, and unfortunately it is still present in football today.

◂◃◆▹▸

Ian Banks played under Barry for Barnsley's youth teams in the late 1970s and the first team in the early 80s. He is considered one of the best attacking players ever to have come through the Oakwell youth system.

MURPH WAS ALWAYS trying to get me to tackle, but that was never going to happen.

You can lead a horse to water but you can't make it drink.

He was one of my main coaches in the first few years of my career and he would get quite frustrated that I didn't get stuck in as much as he used to on the pitch, and that I didn't track back.

That just wasn't my strong point, I was an attacking player.

Murph's whole career had been about working hard and getting stuck in and he couldn't understand why I wasn't that type of player.

I hated tackling and I hated running back, I just wanted to run forward with the ball and shoot or to pass to Ronnie Glavin so he could score.

Murph was just trying to make me into a more well-rounded player but it was never going to happen with me.

I remember there was one game in which, very unusually for me, I won three tackles in about five seconds. I could see Barry laughing, clapping and jumping on the sidelines. I thought… Yeah, I knew you'd like that, Murph.

It probably surprised me even more than it did him.

I first met him when he was coming towards the end of his playing days and I was an apprentice. We used to watch most of the first team games after we played at 11am on a Saturday. You could call him a good honest pro.

What he lacked in talent he made up for in hard work and endeavour.

I have managed and coached myself, and you need people like that in a team. There are wizards and warriors, and Barry was one of the best warriors.

I cleaned his boots a lot.

In those days, the youth team players did everything from 'divoting' the pitch, to collecting kit to cleaning boots… and mopping and brushing the dressing-rooms.

At one point, there was only myself and Graham Reed because it was the end of the season and they had let all the other under-18s players go.

Me and Graham had professional contracts but it meant that, for a few months, we were the only ones who had to clean the entire first team squad's boots every day as well as all the other jobs.

Then, when Barry retired from playing and became a coach, I was in his intermediates team for a year before I got called up for the first team.

I remember going to a tournament in Düsseldorf with the intermediates. It was the first time I had done anything like that. It was a very clean place with great people. We had a great time over there and it was good to represent the club.

The youth teams were very important at Oakwell.

Barnsley had brought through some really good players like Mick McCarthy. They had to do that because they weren't rich and they needed to bring through players from their youth system. They had some phenomenal success with their homegrown players and they trusted people like Barry to bring these players on.

He was soon coaching the first team with Allan Clarke, who would always stand on the sidelines in training while Barry got us working.

Murph was a fitness fanatic and loved putting us through six-mile runs.

We had a lot of success under them and we had a fantastic team with the likes of Ronnie, Mick, Derrick Parker and Trevor Aylott.

I remember the game at Brentford when Allan sat us down and told us that he was going to be leaving, as well as Barry.

It came as a surprise but not a massive one because, when a team is doing well, other clubs come in for the manager and the best players.

They wanted to take me to Leeds.

Barnsley had a free weekend so I was invited by a scout to go to Elland Road and watch a match, then meet Allan afterwards to discuss the move.

I went with my dad and, as we were walking to the dressing-room, we literally bumped into Norman Hunter, who had taken over from Clarkey as the Barnsley manager.

Norman stared at me for a few seconds then opened up on me.

'I know what's going off here,' he told me. 'Get yourself home right now.'

There might have been a few expletives thrown in there as well.

'Dad, come on,' I said.

We went home.

Norman called me into his office first thing on the Monday morning and I thought I was in for a right rollicking.

'I know what they are up to,' he explained. 'I know they want you... but you're not going. Now off you go into training.'

I never heard from Leeds again.

But I have seen Barry over the years. I have played golf with him a few times and seen him in action as a matchday host in the Legends Suite at Oakwell.

He always had a strut in the way that he walked, which he still has now.

He points his toes out.

He always had enthusiasm for football and most of all Barnsley. He's made for the job he has now as club ambassador.

You never could, and still can't, shut him up, so that helps with that role. You can hear him before you see him and that was always the way with Murph.

I like him.

He is very well-liked by everyone and well respected for the person he is and what he's done for the club.

To play 569 games is a fantastic achievement and no one will ever match it.

◄◄◆►►

EVERY DAY, ALLAN sent one of the apprentices out for bacon sandwiches for all the coaching staff. We would all sit around and talk about the latest training sessions and games, and our plan for the weeks ahead.

It felt like the start of something very exciting with Allan at the helm and I was delighted to be involved in it.

Probably the most important figure for Allan was Norman Rimmington, who was officially the physio at that point but so much more than that. He was a real mentor for a young manager like Allan, who would pick Norman's brains all the time about football, the club and the town.

They had an extremely close relationship and I don't think Allan would have had the impact he had at Oakwell if he hadn't had the support and advice of a club legend like Norman.

Allan had good contacts because of the level he had played at.

He brought a lot more quality into the team in Tommy Graham and Derek Bell, but he kept a lot of the players from the Jim Iley era including Ally Millar, Alan Little and Mick McCarthy who, with a first senior season under his belt, flourished even more under Allan.

Of course, we also had a former England striker in Allan Clarke himself. In games, the opposition kicked lumps out of him because he was the most famous player in the division by far.

Everyone wanted to hammer Allan Clarke.

These were Fourth Division players suddenly coming up against an England striker who was a household name. But Allan dealt with it all and played a big part on the pitch.

He was a fantastic example as a player and raised the other players' games a lot. He was clearly coming towards the very end of his career by this point but he still had incredible quality and he proved it in games like the 6-2 Boxing Day win over Port Vale, when he scored a hat-trick.

Allan won his first five games and that just increased all the excitement that his arrival had brought to the club and the town. The crowd for the first home game was more than double the attendance for the last game of the previous season and, after the excellent start, we were getting five-figure crowds for the first time in a decade.

The team was a bit inconsistent but, after throwing away a 4-1 lead at home to Stockport County and drawing 4-4, they were unbeaten in 12 games, including eight wins from nine at one point.

Tommy Graham, Allan and especially Derek Bell were all scoring regularly and we were proving too good for a lot of Division Four sides.

We won 1-0 at Portsmouth which meant that, with two games to go, it would have taken a massive swing in goal average for the teams below us to catch us.

There were 21,000 people for the last home game of the season, when Barnsley beat Grimsby to secure promotion officially. There was a huge sense of excitement about the future of the club.

For me, it wasn't as good as the promotion as a player, which was really something special.

But it was a good achievement for the club.

It was a super season.

THE FOLLOWING SEASON, back in the Third Division, we consolidated and finished in 11th place.

We had some fantastic results, like a 2-0 win at Sheffield Wednesday which was massive for Barnsley fans, but there were bad moments as well.

When we lost 7-0 at Reading in our last game of 1979, Allan was thinking about quitting but Norman Rimmington talked him out of it.

Allan always listened to Norman.

But he knew he needed to make some changes. He called me into his office the next day and told me I was going to become a first team coach and Gerry Young was going to work with the intermediates.

I had already been working with the first team by then, but now it was going to become my full-time job.

Allan knew I was a popular person in Barnsley. I knew the town as well, so I could be a bit of a bridge between him and the fans.

I would like to think he was impressed by my coaching ability as well after the success of the intermediate side. It was a big boost for me to be involved in first-team football and it felt like the right next step in my career.

Myself and Allan had a very close relationship.

He and his family used to come to our house for dinner quite a lot. He would drop his wife and kids off at our house two or three days a week while we were at training.

But my first day as his official first team coach was a very unusual one.

After that 7-0 loss at Reading, he told all the players to report at Woolley Colliery on the Monday morning at 9am.

We all went down the pit with headlamps on and in all the miners' clothes.

'This is where your supporters work to get the money to come and watch you play,' Allan told us all.

'They pay your wages.'

It brought us some fantastic publicity and got us in all the national papers, but I don't think Allan did it for that. He just wanted to show the players how hard the supporters work to pay to watch us play.

For me, I was thinking… *This is what my dad did all his life.*

After going down the mine, the form slowly picked up in the second half of the season and we ended up finishing 11th.

◄◄◆▷►

Joe Joyce was recruited for Barnsley by Barry in 1978 as a teenager. They were both from Consett in the North East. Joyce played for the Reds until the early 1990s, amassing more than 300 appearances. He is now the academy manager at Premier League club Newcastle United.

I AM OFTEN asked… what makes a good coach?

There are a lot of things that go into it but I always put it down to what I learned from Barry Murphy – someone who can inspire confidence and someone who cares. You can have all the technical and tactical knowledge, but the ability to inspire a player, like Barry had in abundance, is the most important thing.

I picked up those lessons from him. It's a game about people and you need to care about people.

I don't think I have come across anyone in football who is better at working with people than Barry. You can still see that now when you see him working at Oakwell in the Legends Suite.

He was responsible for taking me to Barnsley. He still had connections in the Consett area who used to follow local football for him.

One of them told him about me and I was invited to have a trial at Barnsley.

I had been playing for a youth team, my school and a boys' club as well as Durham County Boys, who won a national competition. There were no academies at the time so that was quite a good level.

I had never had a trial at any professional clubs before and didn't expect to make a living out of football. At one point in my teens, I was playing more rugby union than football.

By the time Barry got in touch, I was set to go to university with the plan of becoming a PE teacher.

He knew my parents and made a point of getting their permission.

My mum was a teacher and said I wasn't going anywhere until I had finished my exams at school.

Once they were finished and Barry was still interested, we decided as a family that I would give it one year and see if it worked.

If it didn't, I would go to university.

I was at Barnsley for 13 years and, more than four decades later, I am still involved in football – so it was a good decision.

When I first went down to Barnsley, I stayed with Barry and his wife, Josy and their kids. They made me feel part of the family and very welcome at a time that could have been difficult for an 18 year-old going to a new part of the country.

I always felt Barry took a little bit more responsibility for me because of the North East connection and I always appreciated that.

Going to Barnsley was like moving from home to home, and I know Barry experienced something similar a couple of decades earlier. They were two working class environments with the steelworks in Consett and the coal industry in South Yorkshire.

I just seemed to fit in there.

I soon realised how well-known Barry was in that area after playing for the club for so many years and playing so many games. He was, along with the physio Norman Rimmington, 'Mr Barnsley'.

The warmth that people feel for Barry came out immediately. His enthusiasm, his love of life and love of people is why he has engendered the reputation that he has.

One of my first memories is being on trial and going away with Barry's intermediate side to a tournament in Düsseldorf which we won. It was a great experience for me – who had only played junior football, mainly against local teams in the North East – to suddenly be going away with a professional club and playing sides from overseas, then finishing with the trophy.

We had players like David Speedie and Ian Banks, so there were some real stars in the team and Barry had us well organised with a really good team spirit.

It was a pleasure to go in and train under him because you knew you would have fun. It was tough and he was a hard taskmaster and he put us through a lot of fitness work. But he also knew that, if you didn't enjoy it, you wouldn't perform at your best.

He had some funny sayings like 'different glass'… instead of 'different class' and he used to greet everyone with… 'Aye… Aye'.

He had a little shrill whistle to make everyone aware that he was around to make sure we upped the intensity in training. I can still hear that whistle now.

Barry had a very good relationship with the manager, Allan Clarke, who eventually brought him onto his first team staff at a similar time to when I was breaking into the first team, which helped me a lot.

Allan had come through the Don Revie regime at Leeds.

He was a gentleman and he wanted the best for the players.

He didn't have the same outward enthusiasm as Barry but he had a real love and passion for the game, and a winning mentality. The combination of their personalities worked very well.

My first games for the first team weren't the most prolific performances.

Unfortunately, my first-team debut was in the 7-0 loss at Reading.

I remember sitting on the bench as the goals went in. It has been a standing joke over the years that I went on when it was 0-0, which is funny but not true.

I was a very naive youngster who had never been involved in professional football. I came on believing we could still win but I should have been thinking about damage limitation. That's something I coach into my players now.

If you suffer such a big defeat, it can be really hard to get over.

But Barry was a really strong source of confidence, reminding me I was new to it and telling me what I was capable of, and that I should look at the long-term.

He told me that he had gone through a lot of years of being in and out of the team, which was very reassuring. He was so willing to give advice and he just always made you feel better.

Allan took us all down to Woolley Colliery a couple of days after the Reading game. We got a lift down and then a small train in the mine.

I remember we were split into two groups. One of them included Allan, Barry and the other coaches and some of the senior players. In the other group, there was myself and some of the other younger lads. Phil Chambers used to call us 'the raggy lads'.

The other group walked down their path but, for us, we had to crawl on our hands and knees through puddles.

We got to the coal face and there were two big Barnsley blokes drilling the coal. They stopped and slaughtered us about the game on Saturday, but in a really pleasant way.

Then we crawled back out.

It was a massive eye-opener and it couldn't have failed to have a big impact on us as a team. It showed us what hard work was and that we had it easy compared to them.

I would like to think I had a good work ethic already, due to my upbringing, but that experience just made me work even harder. Every time I walked out at Oakwell and looked over to the old brewery stand, I thought about what most of the men in there had been doing during the week to make the money to watch us.

Later, when the Miners' Strike happened, I felt even more of an affiliation with the people going through that. As a team, we used to go to soup kitchens to help, even though the club had to be seen as non-political at that time.

We used to travel to away games down the M1 past the flying pickets and we'd see police at every service station.

You don't forget those things.

The supporters still came to our games despite it all.

If ever there was a family club, it was Barnsley in the period I spent there.

I loved every minute of the time I spent at Oakwell whether it was good, bad or indifferent. We had some fantastic teams, especially the side from the early 1980s that got up to the Second Division.

I will never forget my time there and the people I met.

I always felt I had a good relationship with the supporters. I used to do a lot in the community, whether it was Wombwell Cricket Lovers' Society or a social club in Monk Bretton. That was probably another influence of Barry's because he knew that was important.

It was a big deal when Allan and Barry left for Leeds United in 1980 but, in terms of succession planning, the board had already identified the next manager in Norman Hunter.

It must have been hard for Barry to leave after all that time.

It was good recognition for Allan and, of course, Leeds was his club.

I was disappointed to see Barry go but I was delighted for him to get the opportunity to coach at such a good level. He kept in touch with me after that and he still does now.

I was sad to leave Barnsley in the end but it's a club I still look out for and I still have friends in the area.

With myself and Barry, there was a full-back from the Consett area in the Barnsley squad for almost three decades from the early 1960s to the early 90s.

But I never came anywhere near matching Barry's record of 569 appearances.

To get that number of games under your belt is incredible and he is in a very small number of players who have done that at any club.

He deserves a lot of recognition and love from the Barnsley public for what he's given to the club over the years.

He played in an era which, dare I say it, was a lot more physical with some very hard tackles but he still managed to play so many games which is a big credit to him.

I owe Barry a lot for what he contributed to both my career and my life. I wouldn't have become a footballer without him.

« CHAPTER 11 »

DURING ALLAN CLARKE'S first two years at Oakwell, the club started to put together what is still known now as one of the best, if not the best, Reds' team ever.

With a mixture of young players from the intermediate teams – like Mick McCarthy, Joe Joyce and Ian Banks – and good signings, including top internationals, Barnsley became a fantastic side which played very good football and went from the Fourth Division nearly all the way to the top flight under Allan, and Norman Hunter.

Norman Hunter was Allan's former Leeds teammate who came in from Bristol City. He had a house in Leeds and a sports shop in Headingley, so it was good for him to move back up to Yorkshire. He also wanted to work with Allan again.

Every day at Oakwell, Norman used to get in a bit early and walk to the end of the corridor where the tea room was to have a cuppa before training. Every morning Nellie, who worked for the club, had a big pot of tea ready for him.

You could set your watch by him.

He was a lovely man and a very good player because he had been there and done it all.

It gave us all a big boost to have another top player and big name playing alongside us, as well as Allan himself.

Norman was an England international who had been in the 1966 World Cup winning squad and he had won a lot of honours at Leeds.

But he was just one of the lads, and you could go to him and talk to him about anything.

You would never have thought he had all the honours he had because he was just so humble and down to earth.

They used to call him 'Bite yer Legs' because he was a little battler of a player. He had a bronze trophy given to him at Bristol City which was a leg with a big bite taken out of it.

At Barnsley he played centre-back and he used to talk and shout at the lads through every game. He was a fantastic asset for the club.

I was extremely sad to hear of his death earlier this year, in 2020.

AFTER THE HAMMERING at Reading, we signed two defenders in Neale Cooper and Ian Evans.

Evans was a big defender and a Wales international.

He was brilliant for us. He had a funny-shaped ankle because George Best had broken it a couple of years earlier, which put him out for two seasons. But he rebuilt his career with us. He made Mick McCarthy when they played together.

Mick was a very young player at the time and Ian brought him on with his leadership. They were both winners and it was a fantastic centre-back partnership, one of the best the club has ever had.

Our attack was very good as well.

We had gone up to Scotch Corner to sign Ronnie Glavin from Celtic.

He met us there and we agreed to sign him. We had no idea how good he was going to be for Barnsley. He had a free role in our team and he was outstanding. The fans loved him and rightly so. He was a fitness fanatic and never wanted to stop training.

He would have loved it in Jim Iley's day.

I used to stay late with him to do extra running. He is considered by many fans to be the club's greatest ever player and I can't argue with that.

Trevor Aylott also came in, in 1979. He was a big centre-forward and a terrific player. He was a southerner but was adopted by the Barnsley fans who absolutely loved him. He scored some very important goals and used to terrorise defenders.

We signed Derrick Parker from Southend in 1980.

In his first training session, I took all the players for the warm-up, then did shooting practice.

I was laying the balls off for all the players. Every single ball Derrick hit went towards the corner flag. We had paid £70,000 for him.

I was shouting… 'WORTH EVERY PENNY!' across the training pitch and everyone was laughing. All the fans behind the goal couldn't believe it because they had come to see the new signing.

But he came good once the matches started. Derrick was a good goal-scorer and he did very well for us.

Aylott and Parker were an excellent combination who worked very, very well together. They were always a threat and scored a lot of goals. Trevor was the big target man, and Derrick just worked around him.

In my era, we had Barrie Thomas and John Evans, who were a good strike force, but Aylott and Parker were playing at a better standard so they have to be the club's best pairing up front.

WHACK.

The sweaty, heavy jersey hit me straight in the face.

It had been thrown by Barnsley's star striker Trevor Aylott in anger after being substituted against Portsmouth in the first game of the 1980/81 season.

You could see Trevor saying 'ME?' after being taken off.

He threw his shirt towards the bench.

It was meant for Clarkey, but it hit me. I just happened to be in the way of it.

I wasn't annoyed with him personally because those things happen in the heat of the moment, but it was disrespectful to Clarkey, who was furious.

Trevor was put on the transfer list and he was fined two weeks' wages.

He had to back down and apologise and, after a bit of a cooling down period, he got back in the team and was a fantastic player for Barnsley again.

◄ ◄ ◆ ▷ ►

Allan Clarke

Barnsley pulled off a major coup in 1978 when they appointed household name Allan Clarke as player/manager. After making his name with Walsall, Fulham and Leicester City, Don Revie paid a British record £165,000 to bring him to Leeds United, for whom he netted more than 100 goals and won both the First Division and FA Cup.

Nicknamed 'Sniffer' for his goal-scoring ability, Clarke also notched 10 goals in 19 games for England, with whom he went to the 1970 World Cup and 1972 European Championship. He led Barnsley to promotion in his first season at Oakwell then, the next year, he returned to Leeds as manager and took coach Barry Murphy with him.

THE SUMMER OF 1978, in which I moved to Barnsley, was a bit of a whirlwind.

I was in my ninth season at Leeds and I was struggling with a knee injury after an operation.

I finally got fit enough to play in a friendly against PSV Eindhoven at Elland Road towards the end of the season and I scored.

All the fans were singing 'Sniffer's back'… but I knew I wasn't back.

I could only get up to three-quarter pace and I had lost my speed which used to scare defenders. I knew I couldn't play in the First Division any more. But I thought I could still do a job as a player/coach at a lower level.

I had wanted to be a manager for a while and I had all my coaching badges. A reporter from a national newspaper rang me one day and told me Ernest Dennis, the chairman of Barnsley, wanted to talk to me.

I went to meet him on a Saturday morning.

Mr Dennis was in the meeting as well as Johnny Steele the general manager. They offered me the manager's job.

I still had two years left on my contract at Leeds and I would have been due a testimonial the next year, but I gave that up to move to Barnsley. I had to take a pay-cut as well.

I would have been picking up cheap money at Leeds, which is not my style. I could contribute a lot more at Barnsley and management was what I wanted to get into.

As soon as I accepted the job, I drove into Barnsley town centre and started talking to shoppers. Some of them recognised me. A lot of them told me they were Barnsley fans but they had stopped going down to Oakwell regularly. I told them I had become their manager and that, if they backed me, I would get them promotion.

They certainly did back me because, by the end of that season, we were averaging about 15,000 every home game which was about four times as many as the previous season.

When I first got the job, it was decided that Barry Murphy and Gerry Young would be my coaches.

Norman Rimmington had been made groundsman by Jim Iley but he wanted to be the physio again. Rimmo was a lovely, lovely man and I called him 'Mr Barnsley'.

It was good to have two Barnsley legends in Murph and Rimmo on my staff – both were very popular with the fans and knew the club inside out. That helped me a lot.

Barry was a very good coach and a very loyal person. He did an excellent job for me. I wouldn't have put him on my coaching staff, and then taken him with me to Leeds, if I didn't think I needed him.

We worked well as a partnership and always got on very, very well.

We were a team. He trained and coached the players on the pitch every day, with me on the sidelines watching and making some changes when they were needed.

My wife and my children used to go to Barry's house a lot and, when the team went away for pre-season, the two wives and sets of children would go away on holiday in a caravan. We all had a very good relationship.

I made quite a lot of changes at Oakwell.

I had learned a lot from Don Revie, who I always call 'the gaffer' after our time together at Leeds. I had ideas about training, tactics and preparation for matches which were quite new to everyone at Barnsley.

I introduced a salt massage every Thursday… me and Norman would do it for every player. That came from the gaffer at Leeds.

The players all loved it.

I looked at Oakwell that first pre-season and thought it was a bit rundown. I told the board that I wanted the ground painted because it was scruffy. The fans came for the first game and the stadium just looked better, which was important.

Eventually I brought in the first disabled access at the ground for people in wheelchairs.

Barry told me that the players didn't go out into the community much and I changed that. I told them they were professional footballers and they represented the club so they should be out meeting the fans, and be proud to walk around the town. They started to do that more at various functions and community events.

Barry always talks about how red-hot on discipline I was with the players. If you don't have discipline in a football club, you may as well pack up and go home. If players were late to training, they were fined.

If they didn't do what I told them, they were fined.

If the players ever stepped out of line, I would come down on them like a ton of bricks.

It was the job of Barry and Norman to act as the peacemakers when the players were upset with me because they thought I had been too harsh with them. Barry was very good with the banter and jokes in the dressing-room and in training, and Norman could calm anyone down if they came to see him in the physio room.

It worked very well like that. They both used to tell the players my bark was worse than my bite and that I was looking after them.

I would always back my players.

In those days, every club used to get tickets for the FA Cup final.

I was in a board meeting and the board members were sharing the tickets out between themselves but I made them give all the tickets to the players. That made the players realise I was the gaffer and I was strict with them, but I would look after them.

Another change I made was that I refused to let the team bus pick Ernest Dennis, the chairman, up from his house on the way to away games. I told him if he wanted to travel with the team, he could come down to the club with the rest of us and get on the bus there.

It was in front of the players, who had never seen anything like this.

They knew who was in charge.

But I did have a lot of respect for Mr Dennis. He passed away while I was on holiday and I came back to go to his funeral. I wouldn't have done that for many people but I always liked Mr Dennis.

I was in every day, even if I had given the players a day off. I saw it as my job to be there all the time and learn how to be a manager. I went out at least two nights a week to watch games.

Barry was always willing to work just as hard as me and I appreciated that.

Instead of playing as a striker, I played in midfield because I could talk to everyone around me and control the game. To play in the Fourth Division was a piece of cake for me.

I inherited a great bunch of lads, then I brought in a couple of good players called Derek Bell and Tommy Graham, who scored a lot of goals. We won the first five matches of the season then we had a blip like every club has, but we got back on track and to get promoted in my first year as a manager was fantastic.

What a lot of people don't know is that, at the end of that season, I had the chance to go to Sunderland, who were competing to get into the top flight.

A man called Arthur Cox, who had been my coach at my first club Walsall, rang me up with a message from the Sunderland board that they wanted me to be their manager. They are a big, big club – who only missed out on getting to the First Division by a point in 1978/79 – and I was tempted.

But, after thinking about it and getting advice off people like Norman and Barry, I decided to reject the offer because I wanted to stay at Barnsley and get some more experience.

I had promised the players that, if they got promoted, we would all go on holiday. I took them back to a hotel in Marbella where I went with Leeds after we lost the European Cup final to Bayern Munich in 1975.

It was worth every penny to take Norman Rimmington on an airplane for the first time, because he was like a little kid – so excited and in awe.

It was marvellous to see.

As for Barry, we found out that he couldn't swim and he refused to sit with us by the pool in case the players threw him in. He used to run upstairs and lock himself in his hotel room.

The next season was more difficult up in the Third Division. We lost 7-0 at Reading at the end of the year.

All the players came off the pitch and went into the bath.

I was absolutely fuming and I told Norman that I was going to quit the job and leave Barnsley.

'You're not going to let that lot beat you, are you? he replied.

I knew he was right.

I went into the room to have a bath and that caused an exodus of the players. I calmed down a bit and didn't say anything on the long trip back except that I wanted them at Oakwell the next day, which was a Sunday.

I told them that, if they played like that again, they would all be looking for new clubs. I also told the board that I was not going to play anymore and that I would just focus on managing.

Then the following day, I took the squad down one of the local pits.

Rimmo's son-in-law worked there and he arranged a visit.

We went down at 6am and the players were all yawning. I told them they didn't know how lucky they were and that these miners worked all week in very difficult conditions to pay their wages.

It got a lot of publicity but it also had a big impact on the players, and I never had another performance like the one at Reading.

In my second season at Oakwell, we had gone through a bad run and we were battling relegation. The board were on my back but I told them they needed to back me to bring in some more players and, to be fair to them, they did.

We brought in players like Ronnie Glavin – who is the best player Barnsley has ever had – and Trevor Aylott and Derrick Parker, who were their best ever strike force.

I think I spent £200,000 on nine players. We had brought through the likes of Mick McCarthy and Ian Banks from the youth system and developed them into cracking players.

I got another job offer the next season and it was my old club Leeds. I decided to take it.

Leeds chairman, Manny Cussins, used to go to the same Italian restaurant as me near Wetherby.

We would talk and he would hint at me getting the Leeds job but I told him that, if he was serious, he would have to go through the Barnsley board, not me. Eventually, that's what he did and I decided to make the move.

Leeds were very close to my heart and it was a massive opportunity to manage at the top level. I took Martin Wilkinson, the chief scout, and Barry with me but Norman Rimmington didn't want to come because Barnsley was his club, which I respected.

For Barry, he had the chance to move to a bigger club and he felt he had to take it. He had had a lot of success with Barnsley at a lower level and he had earned this opportunity.

The Barnsley board asked me who I thought should replace me and I recommended Norman Hunter, my old Leeds colleague who I had signed from Bristol City. Norman had always wanted to be a manager.

Norman Hunter took Barnsley up and I was happy for him but Barnsley fans know that Allan Clarke helped to build that team.

I had had Leeds scouted and we knew they were short of five or six players to stay up.

I said to the board, 'Have I got any money to spend?'

They told me I would have £2 million, which was something to work with. This was just after Brian Clough had made Trevor Francis the first £1 million player.

But, when I got in the job, I didn't have that money.

If they had been honest with me, I would have stayed where I was because I had a better team at Barnsley than at Leeds. Barnsley were definitely a lot fitter and better organised.

With Leeds, I had to work a lot on fitness because they didn't seem to have had much of a pre-season. I said that to the media and Jimmy Adamson, the previous manager, reported me to the FA and I was fined. But it was true.

Myself and Barry had a lot of work to do to get their fitness levels up.

We did well in the first season but the second season was a lot more difficult. We had a board meeting halfway through. I was told there was unrest in the camp and I asked for names, but I wasn't given any. The players were obviously talking to the board.

Those players who did that were cheats and the board should have been helping me to get them out of the club.

The relegation in 1982 was a horrible experience, after everything I had done with the club as a player and everything I wanted to do as a manager.

The Leeds fans know it wasn't my fault and they have never blamed me for it.

It was very hard to be sacked by Leeds and it took me a long time to get over it. I had had ambitions to be very successful with Leeds and then be England manager.

I couldn't ask Barry to leave with me. It was totally fair for him to honour his contract at Leeds.

We haven't seen each other much since but I have been back to Oakwell a few times and Barry has interviewed me in the Legends Suite.

Barry was a massive help for me when I was going into management and I thank him very much for that.

He is a good, loyal man and a fantastic servant to Barnsley FC.

PART FOUR

Leeds United

« CHAPTER 12 »

BARNSLEY WERE TARGETTING promotion in the 1980/81 season and we started quite well, with a good home win over Sheffield United on Yorkshire TV early in the season.

The next home game was also an all-Yorkshire affair and we beat Huddersfield Town 1-0 in what would be my last Barnsley match in the home dugout.

Earlier that week, Allan had called me in off the training ground.

I would normally sit down and talk to him in his office but for some reason, that day, I had a feeling it was about something different so I was standing next to the radiators like a schoolboy in the headmaster's office.

I couldn't believe what he told me.

'Manny Cussins, the Leeds chairman, wants me to go to Leeds,' he said.

I was stunned.

Then he said...'I want you to come with me'.

Leeds had always been the club we talked about as the top level of football, probably with a bit of jealousy but also admiration. When we were running up pit stacks and jogging through woods in pre-season, we used to say, 'I bet they're not doing this at Leeds United'.

They had been in the European Cup final just a few years before in 1975, and were a huge club that was usually competing for the title and trophies.

It was a four-year contract, which is four times longer than any contract I'd ever had. And triple the money I was on at Barnsley.

They were offering a car as well.

Also, it was the chance to work in the First Division which is where I had always wanted to be.

We knew we had to take this opportunity and it didn't take us long to agree to the move. Another lad called Martin Wilkinson, who was the scout, also went to Leeds with us.

Norman Rimmington had the opportunity to come with us, but he didn't want to. Barnsley was his club and he would never leave. Sometimes I wondered whether he wished he had had a taste of the First Division.

We didn't tell the players until we played Brentford down in London on the following Monday. Allan told them before the game in a hotel that we would be going to Leeds. They seemed a little bit disappointed because Allan had done so well.

It was emotional for me, in a big, big way.

I shed some tears in front of everyone because I didn't really want to leave Barnsley in some ways. The club had given me so much and it was very hard to go.

Clarkey gave a speech to the players but I couldn't... I was too emotional. We drew the game 1-1 and the press soon got wind of us leaving and it became a big story.

I HAVE NO regrets.

It was a move I had to make and I would never have forgiven myself if I hadn't done it. I wouldn't want to be in my eighties now thinking... *What if?*... about turning down the chance to go to Leeds.

They were one of the biggest clubs in the country, or even the world, at the time.

If I had stayed at Barnsley, I could easily have lost my job if they decided to bring in a new manager.

The fans thought I shouldn't have gone because of how long I had been at the club. They couldn't understand why I didn't stay and put myself in contention for the manager's job at Oakwell.

Some people fell out with me about it.

I thought that was harsh. I had given more than 18 years of service, broken all the records for appearances and given one hundred percent in every game. But people get used to you and think that a certain club is where you should always be.

They had my face on a dartboard in some local pubs… they were throwing darts at it.

Kids at my children's school, St Michael's, did the same and it wasn't a good time for Louise and Neil. The same thing happened to Paul Heckingbottom in 2018 when he moved to Leeds from Barnsley.

We stayed living in Barnsley. Leeds wanted me to move to a house there but Josy said, 'No'.

Her job as a schoolteacher was much more secure than mine.

Barnsley was my home by then and we decided not to move to Leeds as a family. I would commute.

◄ ◄ ◆ ► ►

Louise Murphy, Barry's daughter and first child was a teenager when Barry moved to Leeds United in 1980.

When my dad was playing for Barnsley, if they lost, it was a difficult journey along the school corridor on a Monday morning.

It was… 'Your dad's rubbish'… and other comments.

It was difficult. I suppose these days it would be called bullying but, in those days, you just had to put up with it.

When he went to Leeds, it wasn't pleasant.

They used to say he was a traitor but, to me, he was just doing the same job at a different place and it was like anyone else moving jobs. I couldn't really see what the problem was but you are a bit naive at that age.

Earlier on, having a dad who played for Barnsley meant that, if we went anywhere, it took a bit longer to do the normal, everyday stuff because people always recognised him.

I couldn't understand what all the fuss was about because, to me, he was just my dad. I thought we were just a normal family.

We used to go to the home games. It was a ritual.

My dad would leave first thing in the morning; then we would all walk down together for the game, with other fans. Then we'd wait for him after the game and go back home. We would watch in a section of the old stand reserved for players' families.

I remember going to his testimonial match and it snowed. I remember the game against Bradford City in the 1971/72 season when there was some crowd trouble, because it was quite frightening. Then I remember the promotion under Allan Clarke and everyone running on to the pitch.

I didn't go to many games when my dad moved to Leeds because I had a Saturday job on Barnsley Market by then.

A few years later, dad used to look after my sons in the summer holidays, when he was at Penistone Leisure Centre, and they have great memories of that. They still talk about it now and my youngest is 26.

I have seen the side of my dad that will do everything for anybody.

He's always been a brilliant dad and now a brilliant granddad as well. We all love him to bits and I don't think he realises how proud of him we are.

◄ ◄ ◆ ► ►

IT WAS A massive national story that Allan Clarke was back at Leeds.

I remember sitting at the press conference table at Elland Road with Allan, Martin Wilkinson and the chairman, Manny Cussins and there were loads of reporters and photographers there.

The next thing we did was walk down to the club shop and introduce ourselves to the staff. There were 15 to 20 of them sending souvenirs to people all over the world who supported Leeds. In comparison, there was maybe one person working in the shop at Barnsley.

Leeds United was a different world to Oakwell.

I realised pretty soon after making the move that I had been living one life as a footballer for my playing career, at a decent level in the Third and Fourth Divisions, but life at the top of the game was totally different.

Your ambition is to get as high as you can in football and I wouldn't have missed it for the world. I was never going to get to the top level as a player but to do it as a coach was the next best thing.

The facilities at the training ground and Elland Road were as good as you could get at that time.

The club had their own restaurant at the ground for the players.

We also had Geoff Ladley who was the England physio at the time.

As soon as you walked into the ground there were lots of pictures of trophy parades and celebrations.

At games, and around the club, you would see so many legendary former players like John Charles, Mick Jones, Peter Lorimer, Bobby Collins and Johnny Giles.

But the main difference was the support. The amount of people who were Leeds fans was overwhelming.

In other ways it was another community club just like the one I had left. The board of directors was made up of local business people just like at Barnsley.

THE PLAYERS WERE a different level.

In the first training session I took, there were 18 internationals.

I had just come from the Third Division and I had never played above that level so I was worried that they might not respect me.

I was a bit nervous but I didn't show it.

I got them running and warming up, and we had a few different routines for them to go through. Then we moved on to the football. I made a few jokes.

I loved it, they loved it and we went on from there.

Allan always used to say that you can't coach players at that level, you just keep them happy and keep them fit.

I wouldn't ask anyone to do anything I couldn't do myself, in terms of fitness. They were all better footballers than I had ever been but, physically, I could keep up with them all and I knew how to organise training sessions and keep their spirits up.

They might have been top level players but they were still just blokes, at the end of the day, so I managed to have a laugh with them and develop good relationships.

It was only me and Clarkey who worked with the first team.

I worked them hard.

The players used to say... 'Will somebody take that bloody stopwatch out of his hand?'

They would take the mickey out of me a bit because I was always putting cones out or collecting them. Sometimes they would hide my cones as a prank.

But they always had respect for me and I got on very, very well with them all because I was myself. What you see is what you get.

PROBABLY THE PLAYER I was closest to was Trevor Cherry.

I knew him very well. We kept in touch ever since we worked together at Leeds, and played golf quite a lot together, so I was devastated to hear of his death this year, in 2020.

He was a fantastic player for Leeds throughout the 1970s and he had just been in the England squad for the 1980 European Championships when we arrived at Elland Road.

He was very good mates with Paul Hart, who went on to be manager of Barnsley. They were inseparable.

Trevor was an excellent defender with good pace and he could read the game brilliantly.

He was a lovely man. He was always willing to listen and learn in training, even though he had already achieved so much in the game. He had a heart of gold and a lovely family.

Another England international at Leeds was Brian Greenhoff, who had arrived from Manchester United the year before. He was a fantastic midfielder and he was from Barnsley so we always had that connection and got on well. He had played in my testimonial at Oakwell five years earlier.

Eddie Gray had been a fantastic player for Leeds, a flying winger who was in their team for 17 years while also playing for Scotland.

There was nobody better than him. If you gave him the ball, he would keep it for as long as he wanted.

Jimmy Adamson, the previous manager, had Eddie in the reserves but myself and Allan got him fit and he was a hell of an asset to the team.

We used him at left-back which he had never played before, but he took to it very quickly. As a former full-back, I worked with him to get him used to the new position. It felt strange being a retired lower league player and giving tips to one of the best footballers in the country, but it was another great experience and Eddie took on board everything I told him. He needed to get used to getting into defensive positions but he was such a clever player that he could adapt to anything.

I had never played with any non-British players.

Then I went to Leeds and they had the likes of Argentinean Alex Sabella and most of the opposition sides in the top flight had at least a few overseas stars.

Jimmy Adamson had only just signed Alex from Sheffield United, where he was a big star.

He didn't speak a lot of English but he knew enough to get by and you could tell he was a fantastic lad.

On the pitch, he was a sensational midfielder with a lot of pace and so much ability it was frightening.

It was a pleasure to work with him and watch him play.

He went on to play for Argentina with the likes of Diego Maradona; then he was their manager in the 2014 World Cup final.

The goalkeeper, John Lukic was a gentle giant at six feet six. He was a smashing lad and a very good 'keeper who would stay on the training pitch when everyone else was finished because he was so dedicated.

When I returned to Oakwell a couple of decades later, John was goalkeeping coach under Andy Ritchie, who had also been at Leeds when I was there.

Byron Stevenson was a Welsh international who played on the right of the midfield. He was a great lad.

Derek Parlane was a Scotland international who was an excellent goal-scorer. I got on very well with him.

We had Terry Connor up front.

He was a young lad at the time and incredibly quick. We used to laugh about how much he would get caught offside. We would say that he was born offside.

Terry was one of the nicest people I've ever worked with in football. He was a local lad from Leeds and his father was a Justice of the Peace in Chapeltown.

He's been Mick McCarthy's assistant manager in various jobs. When Mick was thinking about working with him, I was asked about Terry's character and I couldn't recommend him highly enough.

I AM REALLY pleased that I got to see football at that level and work at some fantastic clubs during First Division games.

For me, coming from Crookhall and Morrison Busty, it was amazing to go to all these world famous stadiums… Highbury, Old Trafford, Anfield… Goodison Park.

The interest in the club was very intense. We used to get interviewed every Friday morning by journalists. Sometimes Allan would do it and sometimes he would send me.

They gave me a big car and free petrol. I used to travel with Maurice Lindley, the scout. We used to go and assess all the opposition.

At first, it all seemed perfect.

Allan had taken over from Jimmy Adamson when Leeds were bottom of the league. They had only won one game all season and none at home.

We took them to ninth by the end of the season and it was a fantastic turnaround.

We had some great results towards the end of the season. We won at Old Trafford against Manchester United, with Brian Flynn scoring the winner. That was the highlight and it was part of a run of six wins from seven games.

We had a fantastic atmosphere and the spirit of the players was superb. They all wanted to win for us.

We were thinking that we were going to bring back the glory days to Leeds United, which was always Allan's ambition.

« CHAPTER 13 »

SOMETHING WENT WRONG in the second season.

Allan started listening to the wrong people, one person in particular who I won't name, who had never played the game but he had a lot of influence all of a sudden. It was never the same after that.

The players, especially at that level, can tell if someone knows about football. Allan would have seen his contract out and been a success if not for that.

I sometimes wonder whether it would have been different if Norman Rimmington had come with us. I am almost certain that it would have been and that Leeds wouldn't have been relegated; and Allan would have seen out his contract.

Norman could calm Clarkey down. He was a mentor.

Norman would have been able to influence him in that second season and make sure he didn't listen to the wrong people.

Allan depended on Norman's advice.

I DON'T KNOW if Allan knew how big a job it was at Leeds. It was a lot to live up to for him. Because he was a member of Don Revie's famous team, he got a bit of extra time and patience but the supporters were used to winning and there was only so long they would put up with not winning.

Even if their hero Allan Clarke was the manager.

We made mistakes in the transfer market. We tried to take Ian Banks with us but it didn't happen.

England player Peter Barnes came in, but it didn't work out.

Allan was warned that Barnes had the heart of a pea. I was out of the country with the youth team but myself and the scouts had told him not to sign Barnes.

Allan had the two best scouts in the league in Tony Collins and Maurice Lindley, but he decided not to listen to them. He listened to other people and signed him.

The club paid £1 million for him.

I came back from my trip away with the youth team and couldn't believe he had signed.

Peter was good on the ball but wouldn't get behind the ball, and do his job for the team. He was a lovely lad and we worked hard with him on the training pitch, but it was a bad signing.

It reminded me of trying to get Ian Banks to do some defensive work.

But that Barnsley team could handle having a couple of flair players who weren't doing much off the ball, whereas this Leeds side – playing in the top flight – couldn't afford that luxury.

The Barnes deal was money down the drain because he could not adapt to a defensive role within the team.

On the first day of the 1981/82 season, we lost 5-1 at Swansea, who had just got back into the top flight. It was a red-hot day and the Vetch Field was packed. They had good players like John Toshack and they were more up for it more than we were. Because we were Leeds United, we thought we had a right to win.

That result was a big shock for us and set the tone for the whole season.

We only won one of our first 10 games and, although we won a few games in late 1980, we slumped again after New Year and were in big relegation trouble.

WE GAVE OURSELVES a chance by bringing in Frank Worthington, who was another England international.

He had been a fantastic player for Leicester City and other clubs. He was in his mid-thirties but still an excellent talent.

We used to do different things in training every day and we always did set pieces on a Friday morning to refresh the lads' memories for the match at the weekend.

We would get the players lined up for a wall so the free-kick takers could practice.

In his first training session, Frank said, 'I take all the free-kicks'.

Every single one in that training session went in the back of the net past John Lukic.

We went to Sunderland the next day and got a free-kick just outside the box late on. Frank curled in the winner.

What a moment.

He was a big character off the pitch.

We had an event at the Royal Gardens and we were all supposed to wear our club suits.

He turned up in a bright pink satin shirt open at the neck to show a big medallion. He had his hair tied back in a ponytail.

That was Frank.

In games, he used to hook the ball over defenders and volley it in.

I once said to him that watching him was like watching Billy Smart's Circus. You didn't know what was coming next. But he was one of the nicest people you could wish to meet.

UNFORTUNATELY, THAT SUNDERLAND game was our only league win from the end of January to the middle of April.

Even though Frank scored nine goals for us, we were struggling to keep them out at the other end and were more or less always in the relegation zone.

We won our last home league game of the season against Brighton and Hove Albion, coming from behind late on after four months without a win at Elland Road, which was unheard-of for Leeds.

We hoped that would be enough but we lost our last game at West Bromwich Albion 2-0. Allan made a couple of changes defensively and they didn't work. We just didn't turn up on the day.

The away crowd erupted.

Leeds supporters can be as passionate as any fans in the world but, that day, they totally turned on us. We were sitting in the dugout at The Hawthorns at the end of the game and there were police horses in front of us trying to get the fans off the pitch.

It was frightening.

West Brom then lost at our fellow strugglers, Stoke City a few days later and that sent us down.

It was less than 10 years after the Don Revie era and it was a massive shock. It was very sad because they are a big, big club and they deserved to be in the top flight.

« CHAPTER 14 »

ALLAN CLARKE WAS sacked at the end of that season.

I was sad to see him go. I got on very, very well with him and our two families were very friendly.

I was told my contract wouldn't be cancelled, which was a relief. I wanted to see out my four years and I felt terrible after the relegation so I wanted to help right those wrongs.

The directors, Bill Fotherby and Manny Cussins took me around the stadium and asked my opinion on who to appoint as the new manager.

I said there was only one man they could appoint and that was Eddie Gray.

I think that persuaded them to make the decision. The fans loved him and he was ready to make the transition to management.

Eddie Gray

A Leeds legend after 17 years on the wing for the Whites. He played under Barry Murphy and Allan Clarke, then kept Barry as his coach when he became manager in 1982.

The thing that struck me about Barry when he first came to Leeds was the enthusiasm he had for the game. He was an infectious character and his love of football rubbed off on people.

I knew about Barry's record at Barnsley and what he had achieved. I knew he held the record for appearances there and for consecutive appearances.

None of us had a problem with working for a coach who had come from the Third Division.

We respected him for the longevity of his career and the way he was on the training pitch and around the club.

He worked very well with Allan Clarke. They were very close at the time and I thought they were a good partnership.

Barry and Allan played me at left-back, which I quite enjoyed.

With Barry being a full-back himself, he would drop me little hints about how to play full-back. You always listen to people, especially people with a lot of experience in the game. I always enjoyed Barry's in-put.

I would get a bit fed up about him constantly talking about how good he was at squash, but he was great fun to be around. He was obviously very keen.

The first season under them was great but we went down in the second season.

It was tough to take but you realise in football that no one has a divine right to be in the top flight.

We just didn't do it that season.

We had a lot of good players but that doesn't always guarantee success.

Allan was quite unfortunate that things didn't work out for him. I know he was very disappointed and I am sure Barry was too.

I was made manager and kept Barry on. We got on well. There was no hesitation in keeping him on after Allan left. Barry was very helpful as a coach and also in bringing through the young players we were developing in that era.

If he disagreed about something, he would tell you. He was very honest, and that's what you want from the people you are working with.

When it came to the end of his contract in 1984, I decided to let him go which was not an easy conversation.

It's always difficult when you have to let anyone go.

But the club had been through a torrid time financially and we had to make a lot of changes. That's the nature of the game. I think Barry was disappointed at the time but, with all his experience, he understood.

I still get on well with him and I like him a lot.

Whenever I go to Barnsley, I go and see him in the hospitality section and it is enjoyable to watch him still talking about football and showing his love for the game.

◄ ◄ ◆ ► ►

EDDIE BROUGHT DOWN Jimmy Lumsden who had been a youth coach at Celtic. The three of us worked with the first team.

Eddie and Jimmy were great to work with and it was a pleasure going around the different grounds with Eddie because everyone in football knew him and respected him.

He brought through a fantastic crop of young players during that time.

John Sheridan was the one player that you could tell, from the first time you saw him play, would make it to the very top. He had stacks and stacks and stacks of ability. He was a lovely player to watch and he could dictate games from the middle of the park with his passing skill. Leeds had brought him in as a teenager from Manchester City. He lacked a little bit of pace but he made up for it by being a very, very clever player.

Scott Sellars was a smashing player as well. He had so much ability in midfield. You could tell he would make it at the top level and I was surprised he never played for England.

Denis Irwin was a great lad but, to be honest, I couldn't see him winning all those Premier League titles with Manchester United in the next decade.

He was a right-back in those days but made it at left-back under Sir Alex Ferguson at Old Trafford. He was a very steady player and clever on the ball but it was touch and go whether he would make it at Leeds because of his defending. Clearly, he improved massively as he got older and had a fantastic career. I am glad about that because he was a lovely lad.

David Seaman was a young goalkeeper who was a very quiet kid from Rotherham. In the end, he was released.

I never would have thought that he would have become England's number one goalkeeper, but he learned a lot at the likes of Peterborough United and Queens Park Rangers before signing for Arsenal, and playing in their famous team of the 1990s.

Tommy Wright, who would go on to be Barnsley's assistant head coach three decades later, was another player who came through the youth ranks.

I knew Tommy very, very well. He was an excellent winger but a tough little character.

They were all on a very short fuse. They had been brought up in the glory days of Leeds United, watching them winning trophies every season and thinking it was hunky dory.

Then suddenly they were getting into the first team, but Leeds were in the Second Division.

I used to take charge of the youth teams and I took them to competitions throughout Europe. We went to Pula in Croatia, with a team including Denis Irwin, Scott Sellars and Tommy Wright. It was a fantastic competition which lasted nearly a fortnight and included Barcelona and Juventus.

It's a great place and I took Josy back there soon afterwards.

We walked into a bar and the man pointed at me and shouted... 'Leeds United!' because he recognised me.

DESPITE HAVING SOME really good young players, Leeds couldn't get the results they wanted under Eddie.

There was an expectation that we would come straight back up but we finished eighth in the first season in Division Two and tenth the next season.

We started well in the 1982/83 season and were near the top of the league but we fell away from the middle of the campaign.

We played against Arsenal in the FA Cup in 1982/83 and there were two replays. We drew down at Highbury; then we were winning at Elland Road but we drew 1-1. The Gunners won the second replay 2-1 but we had shown we could compete with a top team.

The next season, we had some bad moments, like a 5-1 loss at Shrewsbury Town and also an eight-match winless run. We were even in danger of dropping into the Third Division at one point which would have been unthinkable, but eventually we finished in mid-table.

Eddie had great knowledge of the game but couldn't get as much control over the team, whereas Allan Clarke was the other way around. I always say that the discipline of Allan Clarke and the football knowledge of Eddie Gray would have made the perfect manager.

BY THE TIME Leeds were relegated into the second flight, Barnsley had been promoted from the Third Division under Norman Hunter who had taken over from Allan Clarke as manager.

Going back to Barnsley with Leeds was pretty bad and a funny feeling for me. You work at one club for so long; then you're working against them. I always want Barnsley to win but I was employed by Leeds so I wanted them to win at Oakwell.

I never really got any boos or abuse from the fans, which was good.

It was strange because I was still living in Barnsley and I knew so many people at the club and in the stands.

The first time we went back, in November, 1982, there was a huge crowd of more than 21,000. It was the first meeting of the two clubs in 27 years.

It was one of my old youth players who did all the damage. Winston Campbell put Barnsley ahead with a diving header and then, after we equalised, he won a penalty which Ronnie Glavin converted for a 2-1 win.

I was invited back to Oakwell in 1983 to play in the testimonial of my old teammate and friend, Phil Chambers.

I also came back with Leeds the next season in October and we won 2-0 with a couple of late goals. But it was an ugly match in which several players came off injured, including John Sheridan who broke his leg.

One of the only things I truly regret in my career is celebrating Peter Barnes' goal in that game.

I just leapt off my seat in the dugout and jumped around with my arms up.

I shouldn't have done it. It was disrespectful to a club I spent 20 years with.

I was caught up in the emotion of the goal because I was focused on my job at Leeds and we needed to win the game but, in hindsight, I should have stayed on the bench.

There aren't many things I would change in my career, but that is one of them.

We also lost at home to Barnsley in 1984. We had won the previous five games so it was a bit of a shock. Tommy Wright put us ahead but Glavin equalised, then

David Johnson got the winner.

That night, I played in a squash league in Barnsley and got a bit of stick from everyone there – thankfully, I won my match.

HOOLIGANISM WAS A big problem in the 1980s.

Leeds had a very bad reputation for violence in the fan base. They had to shut stands at Elland Road sometimes because of the behaviour of the supporters.

It was just a small core of fans who were vicious.

Everywhere you went with Leeds there was trouble, with their fans and the opposition fans.

We were going down to Birmingham City once and there were Blues' fans standing on a bridge at Spaghetti Junction throwing bricks down at the team bus. It was scary. The bus got damaged but none of us were injured. We would try to get to away grounds early, or take a different route, to avoid things like that.

We went to Queens Park Rangers and played on their plastic pitch. There was fighting in the stands and the police horses were charging across the pitch, which made a very loud noise. Again, it was frightening.

Violence in the stands was a big problem in football back then.

AT THE END of the 1983/84 season, after Leeds had finished tenth, Eddie Gray told me my contract wouldn't be renewed.

It was one of the worst days of my life.

I never saw it coming at all.

I knew my contract was coming to an end but I assumed that Eddie would keep me on in some role, even if it was slightly different to my previous one.

We had been at a reserves match the previous day, at Derby County; then the players had a day off. I was in early as usual and Eddie called me into the office. I sat down and thought he was going to talk about football or signings.

'Barry... I am not renewing your contract!' he said bluntly.

He said the reason was that he was bringing in some other staff for the first team and he didn't think I would want to be moved back to the reserves.

He knew I would always want to be involved in the first team and it just wouldn't work. I understood what he was saying but I was devastated to leave Elland Road.

I went into the dressing-room and said to some of the players. 'Well… that's me gone!'

They couldn't believe it.

It hurt me a lot.

It broke my heart to leave Leeds.

I travelled back in my car and I was very upset; I don't know how I got back because I couldn't really concentrate.

I turned on the TV and it was on the headlines on the news… *"Barry Murphy sacked at Leeds"*.

Josy and I went out to Keresforth Hall in Barnsley to take our minds off it. The well-known actor, Stan Richards, who played the game-keeper Seth Armstrong on *Emmerdale Farm*, was in there as he was a regular.

To cheer me up, he did a drawing of himself kicking a ball with a note saying… 'There's nowt to this footballing lark. Keep your chin up'.

We still have it on our wall at home.

Leeds were fantastic with the compensation they gave me. They looked after me, as I had looked after them.

I would never have a bad word to say about Leeds.

It's just a shame that things didn't go better on the pitch.

PART FIVE

Moving On

« CHAPTER 15 »

AFTER LEAVING LEEDS, I was really down... and remained down for about six months. It was one of the toughest times of my life.

I had never been on the dole until then.

I used to have to go down to the Job Centre and sign on to get my money. They would ask me what area of work I wanted to apply for, but I knew that no jobs in football would be on their lists.

The first time I went to sign on, there was a young girl working there.

She was asking me questions about the jobs I was looking for. I told her I had been a football player, and then a coach at Leeds United.

'Can't you get another job like that?' she asked me.

It was frustrating.

I did that for a couple of months and I was getting quite desperate for a job.

It wasn't like modern football, when people get massive pay-outs, especially from top flight clubs. I had reached the end of my contract and I didn't have a wage anymore.

It was worrying.

ALL I KNEW was that I didn't want to go back into professional football full-time.

I had been at the top with Leeds and I felt nothing would get better, unless it was the Barnsley job which had gone to Bobby Collins earlier in the year after Norman Hunter left.

After I left Leeds, I got a few offers to be manager of other clubs.

A man called Brendan Elwood, who was the Stockport County chairman, offered me the job there but I turned it down. Sheffield FC, the world's oldest club, also wanted me to be their manager.

Their chairman picked me up in a Rolls Royce and took me to Sheffield for an interview, and all the local press were there, looking for the story. I thought about it but I didn't want to go down to non-league football. My heart just wasn't in it.

I felt I had finished at the biggest club in Leeds.

I had done everything I wanted to do in the professional game and didn't want to be involved in it anymore on a full-time basis. It was partly because of the way it had finished at Leeds which was really disappointing.

Eventually something else came up.

I got a job as a sports development officer for Barnsley Council, along with my former Barnsley teammate, John Peachey. Our role was to go around all the sports and leisure centres in the borough and improve them, while also putting on courses.

It was a big change of pace from being a coach at Leeds United just a few months before, but I was still involved in sport and without the intensity of professional football. It was a good job and doing that work helped me move on from what happened at Leeds.

I HAD MANAGED to get a new job but a lot of people in the town were out of work.

Barnsley was a big centre of the Miners' Strike in 1984/85 because it was where Arthur Scargill was based and the borough had a lot of pits in it.

It didn't affect me personally in terms of my job but it had a massive impact on the town. I knew a lot of people who lost their jobs and it split families up, because some broke the picket lines and their relatives never spoke to them again.

I had been on the dole for a few months the previous year but I couldn't imagine what the miners and their families were going through.

It was very close to my heart because my dad was a miner and it could easily have been me on strike, if I hadn't made it in football. Lots of mines had already closed in the North East when I was playing for South Shields and a lot of those folk came down to Barnsley for work.

They used to call certain areas of Barnsley 'Geordie Villages' because there were so many of them living and working there.

The strike had a huge impact on the town and people still talk about it a lot today. Some areas of the borough still haven't recovered.

It was a sad time.

I believe what the club should have done was to let the striking miners in to games for free, or at least half price.

It would have been a fantastic PR move but, more importantly, it was the right thing to do. The miners could have brought proof that they were on strike.

I am sure it was suggested to the club but, for some reason, it never happened.

It was a big mistake not to do that.

At the end of the day, those people had been keeping the club going for decades and decades with the money they had paid at the turnstiles to see the team. The least the club could have done was let them keep coming to games in their hour of need.

I am not sure who made that decision at Oakwell, because I wasn't involved with the club at that time, but it was an error.

Attendances went down because the fans just didn't have the money.

I played in some charity matches, along with some other former Barnsley players, to raise money for the miners who were out of work.

I had my own charity side that raised money for various causes.

We had a team called… Barry Murphy All-Stars. It was a team of current and former players as well as fans, and we played against local teams to raise money for local charities. Emlyn Hughes – the England and Liverpool legend – played in some of the games.

The pub teams used to kick the hell out of us.

We raised about £5,000.

I ENJOYED MY time as a sports development officer but there was only funding for a two-year project.

After that, I moved to Penistone Leisure Centre on a contract of 21 hours a week.

I was due to start on a Monday.

I had seen in the *Barnsley Chronicle* that there was an antique fair there on the Sunday so myself and Josy went up to have a look at the place.

It was an absolute dump and I thought to myself… *Well, it can only go one way.*

As we were coming out, Josy turned to me.

'You're never going to go in there and work!'

I said, 'I will…'

'I'm going to get it going.'

It wasn't what I had been used to at Leeds or Oakwell but I loved every minute of it.

I spruced the place up.

I put hanging baskets and decorations up; I painted the floors and the walls, and I had walls removed to make it into a bigger and better space.

When it rained, I used to have to get up on the roof and brush the water off.

I used my tools and skills from being a tiler to make some repairs up there.

When I started, there was nothing going on but, not long after, there wasn't a spare hour in the day.

We did every sport you can think of for under-fives to over-85s.

Every minute of the day there was something going on – bowls, badminton, football, circuit training, aerobics, first aid courses, exercises for older people or gym sessions for disabled people.

There had been plans to close the centre, but it became the most popular facility in the borough. It was making a lot of money for the council.

They used to call it 'Penistone drill hall' but I made sure everyone called it a sports centre or leisure centre. I spent nearly all of my time up there.

I was on a two-year contract for 21 hours a week, then it went up to full-time.

Sports development officer was my official title but, really, I was a jack of all trades. There were one or two full-time staff there, as well as other instructors who we brought in for the various sports.

I had a budget and all the instructors' fees came out of that.

I was desperate to get Penistone Sports Centre in the *Barnsley Chronicle* every single week to keep up publicity and make sure people kept coming to our sessions. So, I used to do presentations to instructors for the 'Best Class of the Week' with a box of chocolates. They were all completely made up… just so that we would get a picture in the paper.

I worked my socks off but the satisfaction I got was fantastic. It was very different to professional football, but just as enjoyable.

I ALSO INTRODUCED 'Barry Murphy's coaching sessions' and I did three men's circuit training sessions per week.

I looked the part with my tracksuit, and I played the part well because I had a lot of experience in professional football.

I used all the drills, techniques and skills I had picked up during my time at Barnsley and Leeds. There were people queuing out of the door. A chap used to come from Grantham for my circuit training sessions.

It was the hardest circuit training you could get. The sessions were only supposed to be for about 30 people so, if more than that turned up, I would make them extra hard so people would drop out. But it didn't really work.

My name attracted a lot of people and I managed to get the likes of Ron Atkinson to take guest sessions. Yorkshire County Cricket Club and England players, Martyn Moxon and Arnie Sidebottom put on cricket coaching classes.

I trained Penistone Church FC in pre-season in the evenings, after working at the sports centre in the day. It was the first time they had had pre-season training.

They put floodlights up for me so that I could train them in the evenings. They're doing fantastically well now and are one of the top teams in the area.

Dave Hampshire
Penistone Church are now one of the top non-league clubs in Yorkshire but, in the late 1980s, they were playing in the Sheffield County Senior League. Dave Hampshire was club secretary.

Back in the mid-1980s, the club was doing okay, but it was a typical amateur club and we struggled to get people to commit to it.

One of the lads who helped run the club said that we needed to get someone like Barry Murphy in to take training. Not many were coming to training. They were working, or their wives wouldn't let them out.

Several of us knew Barry from Penistone Leisure Centre so we asked him, and he was up for it.

Within a week, the numbers doubled. It was infectious.

Because it was Barry Murphy from Barnsley Football Club, it was a really big deal. But people kept coming because they enjoyed it. Before then, we had just gone for runs in training but he made it all about football and skills and set pieces, as well as our fitness.

It was always a laugh.

Sometimes your stomach ached just as much as your body ached because of the laughter.

He always made it interesting and entertaining. He would tell us that someone at the sports centre had done a certain number of a drill, and challenge us to beat that number.

Everybody loved Barry, he was spot on.

He had a great knack of making sure you enjoyed something that was really, really hurting your body. You had to work hard, but you had a laugh as well.

He would always be taking the mickey out of someone, but in a friendly way.

Our fitness improved and our results improved. We got a lot of new players out of it as well because so many local footballers wanted to train under Barry Murphy.

He didn't come to the matches because he was scouting on weekends, but he would talk to our manager and work on the things we needed to work on, which would be implemented in games. He wasn't there on the matchdays but his influence was there.

He got us to put some floodlights up on the training area. We got some big scaffolding poles with lights on top. They have been replaced since but they are still in the same place, so Barry started the improvement in our facilities.

He raised the profile of the club because not many teams around our area at that level had a former professional footballer taking their training sessions.

We would always go to the pub after training and he would tell us so many stories about his time at Oakwell and with Allan Clarke at Leeds, which were great.

He brought in a better standard of how we should behave. We were an amateur club but he instilled a professional attitude into the players. He had been at Barnsley and Leeds and was a scout at Nottingham Forest at the time, so the professionalism from those places rubbed off on us.

That professionalism he brought in has never gone away and it's ingrained in the likes of me and other people at the club — even down to little things like cleaning the dressing-room after every away game, and making sure we look smart when we arrive for matches.

We didn't have a junior side at our club before 1987 but Barry heard about a coach who wanted to start an under-16s team and he suggested they be based at Penistone Church, and found someone to provide the kit.

That was the first kids' team we had and, from then on, we have built it up to now having a team at every age group from under-7s to under-18s, with two sides in some of those age groups.

He was loved by everybody at our football club and everybody at the leisure centre, and in the town.

People were so proud to go to Barry Murphy's training sessions, whether they were young kids or pensioners.

In his junior sessions at the sports centre, he would get the kids to play for prizes like a Mars Bar, a bag of Monster Munch or a bottle of Coke. I think he must have had shares in Mars because he seemed to give one away every day.

He would finish his training sessions with a competition to hit the crossbar. This was years before the 'Crossbar Challenge' on Soccer AM. Barry could claim to have invented that.

Almost all the players we had at our club in the decades after Barry worked in Penistone had been to his sessions as kids, so they all came with the right attitude. A lot of our players even now will have been to a session with Barry Murphy when they were younger, and most of the fans will have as well.

There are some good stories about him. One of the young lads who used to go to his coaching sessions used to get lifts home with Barry afterwards. Barry always dropped him off in a village called Silkstone, because that's where he thought the lad lived, but he actually lived in Cawthorne which is about a mile and a half away... so he used to run home on the back lanes.

He never told Barry because he was too shy to reveal to this Barnsley legend that he was dropping him off in the wrong place.

Barry used to take the kids he trained on trips to professional clubs like Manchester

United, which they loved. I went with him a couple of times. He had them all under control because they looked up to him and respected him.

He took them to Nottingham Forest to meet Brian Clough.

He did a lot for local lads, taking them to trials at professional clubs if he thought they had potential. Sometimes it was Forest, who he worked for, but other times it was lower clubs who were more their level.

Barry was fantastic for us as a club and for Penistone in general. He had a positive impact on the lives of so many people and he is one of the best men you could meet.

◄◄◆►►

IN THE SCHOOL holidays, I was the mothers' favourite.

We put on sessions every day of the six weeks from 10am and there would be 30 or 40 of them knocking on the door from 8.30am.

Some of the kids just wanted to come and wear the strip; they couldn't really play football but they enjoyed it and that's what it was all about for me.

Some of them were fantastic talents.

John Stones, who would go on to sign for Manchester City for £50 million, and future Barnsley captain, Marc Roberts both came to my junior classes.

Before them, there was the likes of Chris Morgan, who is from Penistone and went on to play for Barnsley in the Premiership.

I met John Stones a few years ago and he said to me, 'Ey up Barry… do you remember me?'

Marc Roberts said the same to me. I had to admit I didn't remember them from when they were kids… they had been about three foot shorter and I had trained thousands of people by then.

I'm glad they had a good time at my sessions and that they've gone on to do so well in the game. I took the boys on trips to Manchester United and Leeds United for football sessions. People stop me in Barnsley to talk about those days almost as much as they do to talk about Barnsley FC.

I USED TO wear squash shoes to do everything but I kept wearing them down because they had a very thin sole. I went into a sports shop in Barnsley to buy a new pair.

The woman in there said that I shouldn't really be wearing those shoes to take part in a fitness class and that I should tell the instructor.

'I am the instructor,' I told her. 'I'll take them… size eight, please!'

That was that.

I ALWAYS KEPT abreast of what was going on at Oakwell, but I could only watch Barnsley when I was sent there as a scout.

They were promoted to the Premier League in 1997.

It was marvellous for Barnsley. I had kept in touch with a lot of people there and the manager Danny Wilson.

My old friend Big Eric had done a fantastic job bringing through all the young players like Nicky Eaden, David Watson and Adi Moses, and then he became Wilson's assistant.

I felt over the moon going up from the Fourth Division, so I couldn't imagine what it felt like to be in that team that got to the top flight.

John Dennis was the chairman and his father, Ernest had been the chairman during my playing career. It was fantastic for the town which had been through a lot of difficult times with the Miners' Strike and unemployment.

When people asked who I had played for, I said Barnsley and since they were in the Premiership most people knew who they were.

After the promotion, BBC and ITV news cameras came up to the sports centre to speak to me as a long-serving former player.

I was very happy for the club but I was also delighted that my sports centre was getting coverage on television and I would give it as many plugs as possible.

It said, "Barry Murphy, Penistone Leisure Centre" on the label for the interview – I made sure of that.

I stayed at Penistone for more than 15 years until I retired in 2002.

I built it up from nothing and, as sentimental as it might sound, it helped build me back up after everything that happened at Leeds.

The community runs it now and it's still a great facility.

« CHAPTER 16 »

AS WELL AS my work in Penistone, I was still working in professional football as a scout.

Blackburn Rovers manager, Bobby Saxton got in touch with me when I finished at Leeds. He got my number off Leeds and called me.

He was a big name in those days and he wanted me to work with him as a coach at Blackburn. I had had enough of coaching, so I turned him down.

But I told Bobby I would be his scout on the weekends. Scouting kept me involved in the game which is all I wanted.

Everywhere I went, I was sitting in the directors' box.

It was a part-time role, going to different matches and producing reports on players. I did Third and Fourth Division games across the north.

I said to myself… *It's pointless going to the First and Second Division because they're all good, well-known players.*

I wanted to look at the lower leagues, where young apprentices were coming through and trying to make a name for themselves.

You have a better chance of being able to afford them.

I travelled all over and I enjoyed it.

I wrote the reports on paper and Josy typed them up. It looked very professional.

IN 1985, BOBBY Collins left Barnsley and I applied for the job. But they gave it to Allan Clarke.

Geoff Buckle was the chairman and he was a big mate of Allan's.

Clarkey was still such a big name at the time and he had been really successful the first time at Barnsley, so it was always going to be difficult to compete with him.

I was very disappointed not to get an interview, however. I just got a letter back thanking me for my application.

The only full-time job I would have taken in football was the manager's job at Barnsley.

THERE WAS ONE other awkward moment at Oakwell.

I went there to watch Barnsley's opposition as a scout for Blackburn. Normally, there would be tickets waiting for me. But, this time, one official wouldn't let me in because he said I had watched Barnsley enough.

I wasn't even watching them!

I was watching the opposition. So, I had to pay to go in and watch the game from the terraces. I was a bit upset because I never thought I would be turned away at Barnsley. Other scouts who saw what happened couldn't believe it.

The chief scout from Blackburn came across and gave the man a real rollicking.

AS WELL AS scouting players, I would also watch opposition teams who Blackburn would be playing in the near future and compile reports on them.

Once I watched a game at Shrewsbury and told them to be aware of the goalkeeper running to the edge of the box to throw the ball out.

Bobby Saxton told the players what I had told him; one of them intercepted the ball and scored. It was pleasing when things like that happened, because you knew you could still contribute.

I would provide details down to which way the goalkeeper dived for penalties. It's easier now because they have video clips but, in those days, teams relied on the scouts.

Bobby Saxton left Blackburn, then moved to York City in 1987 and I scouted for them too.

I enjoyed my time at York. It was a lower level but it was a good, family club not too far from where I lived.

But eventually I moved on again.

ALAN HILL, MY former Barnsley teammate who was then on Brian Clough's staff at Nottingham Forest, invited Josy and I down to a charity football match in Nottinghamshire.

We went to Alan's pub first which had a big garden in it.

Clough was there, telling us how to look after sweet peas which were growing nearby.

We didn't go to the match, we stayed in the pub with Cloughie and his coaches, Ronnie Fenton and Archie Gemmill.

Alan had invited me there to offer me a job as a scout for Forest.

Brian Clough jumped in.

'You've worked in the top flight with Leeds United… you've worked at Blackburn Rovers, and now you're at York City in the lower leagues.

'You should be at a higher level… come and work for us.'

So, I did.

I met Cloughie a few times. He spoke his mind a lot and you respected him for what he had achieved and who he was.

I was once with Alan Hill and Ronnie Fenton when they were picking a reserves team. Clough came in and I asked him if he wanted me to leave.

'If they don't want you to leave… I don't!' he told me.

They used to call all the scouts down from all across Britain four or five times a year for a weekend. Brian Clough always gave us a speech.

One year, some scouts from Ireland who had found Roy Keane for the club were present and Cloughie was encouraging us to find another player like him.

That was a big ask.

AS A SCOUT, you're just recommending players and you don't have any control over whether they get picked up or not.

It's about being in the right place at the right time, like I was with Morrison Busty when a scout came to look at someone else.

If Forest had been tipped off about a player, or several players, from a certain team, they would send me but not tell me who I was looking at. 'Just tell me who catches your eye,' Ronnie Fenton would say.

If I came up with the same names that had been recommended, they would take it further.

I recommended Trevor Sinclair for Forest when I saw him playing for Blackpool as a 16 year-old. At the time he was on the ground staff and mainly playing in the reserves.

Me and Josy went to Blackpool for two days and I dragged her to Bloomfield Road to watch a game. Sam Allardyce was the Blackpool manager at the time.

I told Forest to go and get Sinclair but it didn't happen.

It would have been a good signing because he went on to play for England. He famously scored a spectacular overhead kick for Queens Park Rangers against Barnsley in the FA Cup. I reminded people at the time that I had seen him play when he was 16 and knew he was a top player.

I also recommended Andy Cole when he was playing for Bristol City. Unfortunately, Forest decided not to sign him which was probably a mistake because, a year later, he signed for Newcastle United and became one of the top scorers in the Premier League.

◄ ◁ ◆ ▷ ►

Alan Hill

A goalkeeper for his hometown club Barnsley from 1960 to 1966, and a former Oakwell colleague of Barry's. Alan later spent 25 years at Nottingham Forest, mainly as a coach and scout, during which time they won the European Cup. He hired Barry as a scout in the 1980s.

I met a lot of fantastic people in football, and Barry was one of the very best.

In the late 1980s, I got him a job as Nottingham Forest's scout in the South Yorkshire area. I knew he already had some experience in scouting and would do a good job with us. He was there at the time we had success with two League Cup wins and an FA Cup final.

He mainly did scouting reports on the opposition.

He was very good at it and dedicated. He would go wherever we wanted and, like with everything in his career, he would do a good job.

I have known Barry since he first signed for Barnsley in the early 1960s.

I had joined straight after I left school in 1958; then I signed a professional contract in 1960 and made my debut that year when I was 17 because the two senior goalkeepers both had the flu.

I then spent a lot of time in and out of the side because I had problems with my shoulders which kept dislocating. Eventually I moved on to Rotherham United in 1966. I didn't want to go but the chairman, Joe Richards told me the club needed the money to survive. They sold me for £12,500 which was a lot of money at that time.

That was the time when Barnsley were really struggling financially and they nearly folded the next season. I was going up a level to the Second Division but it was still disappointing to leave my hometown club. I am still a Barnsley fan and I love the club.

I had three years at Rotherham, then moved on to Nottingham Forest. I played 41 games in the First Division but then broke my arm in four places against Everton which finished my career. I got a testimonial and they offered me a job as a youth coach.

I worked in the academy, then I was chief scout. I was assistant manager under Frank Clark in the 1990s.

I worked with Brian Clough for 18 years which was a fantastic experience. He was a brilliant man.

When I first became head of youth development, I went in to see him about coaching. He said, 'Don't talk to me about coaching. Football is a simple game and it is people like you who make it difficult.

'Goalkeepers stop the ball from going between the two posts... full-backs defend... centre-backs head the ball... preferably away from my goal.

'Midfielders pass the ball or give it to someone who can... wide players cross the ball... strikers score.

'That is coaching and so is this... get your hair cut!'

Cloughie was one of football's best characters, and so was Barry.

My best mate when I played for Barnsley was George Kerr, who lived in digs on Dodworth Road with some other players, including Barry. With some players, you think... he's full of himself... but Barry was the sort of person you took to straight away.

We became friends very quickly.

We lived on the same road eventually, Robert Avenue in Cundy Cross. He is one of the few people I have managed to keep in touch with from that era at Barnsley, along with George Kerr and Eric Winstanley. The four of us used to go out together and spend a lot of time together socially.

I have some good photographs from that era with lots of players in them, including Barry.

I didn't play a lot with him but, whenever I did, he wanted to win and he was a great person to have in your team.

I used to admire him as a player; he was determined and he was a leader.

Anyone who came into the club, he always made them feel welcome and he was the kind of person you want at a club.

When I left the club in 1966, Barry was still bouncing from the first team to the reserves and he wasn't a regular player.

I definitely didn't think he'd go on to make more than 550 appearances for the club and be the all-time record holder for games played.

But I did know he would have a good career with the attitude he had.

What he achieved with Barnsley was fantastic. He was an outstanding servant to that club.

He was very lucky that he didn't have many injuries but he deserved all that luck because he is a lovely man who I have always respected.

◂◁◆▷▸

I WAS AT the FA Cup semi-final between Forest and Liverpool in 1989, which is now known as the Hillsborough Disaster in which 96 people died.

Myself and Josy were invited as guests of Forest.

Earlier we had walked past the part of the stadium where the tragedy would happen and we could see there were a lot of people outside looking for tickets. It was very, very crowded.

Josy said straight away, 'It's getting busy behind that goal'.

I told her to watch the game, thinking everything would be okay.

Then a few minutes later they all spilled onto the pitch. We saw Forest fans take an advertising hoarding off to use as a stretcher and run to the injured fans. We were ushered inside and they kept giving us updates.

It was incredibly sad and frightening and it haunts me to think about it to this day.

We went back to Barnsley through a village called Oughtibridge. There were Liverpool fans parked up and using the phones in the houses of local people as they tried to find out what had happened or tell their families that they were okay.

No one knew exactly what had happened at that point, but we started to hear bits and pieces on our way home; then we found out more on the news.

Our son, Neil was also at the game, in a different part of the ground, and we were worried about him at first but we found out he was fine.

That was the one really, really bad day of my time in football.

Relegations and being sacked feel like the end of the world at the time but they are nothing compared to moments like that. Football has given me my whole life and my career but that was a bad day when it suffered a real tragedy.

I ENJOYED THE final part of my career when I was working in Penistone during the week and scouting at the weekend.

I had the best of both worlds.

The Forest coaches knew the number of the leisure centre and they used to ring for me there to tell me which games to go to that evening or weekend.

I retired from the leisure centre and carried on scouting for a couple of years.

Then Peter Ridsdale, the Barnsley FC director, asked to speak with me.

Patrick Cryne had recently saved the Reds from folding, which reminded me of nearly four decades earlier when we nearly went bust.

They were rebuilding.

The club was introducing an executive experience at Oakwell on matchdays and they wanted a former player to oversee it and talk to the supporters.

Gary Megson was phasing out the scouts at Nottingham Forest. I decided to stop scouting and take that job at Barnsley.

At the start of the 2004/05 season, I was appointed as club ambassador and, since then, I have attended nearly every home match in the Legends Suite.

The next two Barnsley managers, Paul Hart and Andy Ritchie had both been my players at Leeds. I had plenty in common with them.

There have been lots of managers since then and some big highs and lows on the pitch.

I LOVE MY role at the club.

People know me. I know I will only get recognised at one ground in the country which is Oakwell.

I love watching the games as well.

I have to give a little speech about the match after the final whistle.

If it's been a bad game, a lot of people say, 'I don't know what you're going to say about that, Barry'.

I never crucify the team because I have been a player and know what it's like. I don't go into tactics when I give my little speeches after the games, and I always try to stay positive.

The game is much better now.

I often wonder what it would be like to be a player now rather than in my day. But, looking back over my life and my career, I am glad it has turned out exactly as it has.

I have loved my time in football and hope you have enjoyed reading about it in this book.

Barry,
You Reds!